Building Powerful Children

Raising a Generation That Will Shape the Future for God

A Practical Biblical Guide for Parents, Teachers, and Leaders to Nurture God's Next Generation

Gerard Assey

Building Powerful Children:

Raising a Generation That Will Shape the Future for God

A Practical Biblical Guide for Parents, Teachers, and Leaders to Nurture God's Next Generation

By
Gerard Assey

Published by:
Gerard Assey
19/18, Palli Arasan Street
Anna Nagar East
Chennai - 600 102

ISBN: 978-81-993017-5-7

Table of Contents

Preface

Every generation stands at a crossroads. One path leads to compromise, confusion, and corruption—the other to courage, conviction, and Christlike character. The future of families, churches, and nations depends on which direction our children take. Yet that direction is not decided when they are grown—it is determined long before, often in the quiet, unseen moments of childhood.

This book: ***'Building Powerful Children: Raising a Generation That Will Shape the Future for God-*** *A Practical Biblical Guide for Parents, Teachers, and Leaders to Nurture God's Next Generation"* was born out of a deep stirring in my spirit as I observed the increasing darkness and moral drift in today's world. The enemy has always known the power of the seed—the next generation. From the time of Pharaoh's decree to destroy the Hebrew infants, to Herod's massacre of male children in Bethlehem, Satan has repeatedly targeted children because he fears their potential. He knows that within every child lies the promise of deliverance, the hope of revival, and the seed of God's Kingdom purpose.
Sadly, while the forces of darkness begin their work from the womb, much of the Church often begins too late—focusing on reaching youth when the foundations have already been formed. This must change. God is calling His people to *refocus* on the young—to build, nurture, and empower children who will not just survive the world, but transform it for His glory.

As I prayed over this burden, the Lord impressed upon me the word **F.O.C.U.S.** — an acronym that became the framework for this book:

- ✓ **F – Formative Years Matter:** *Building from the foundation up.*
- ✓ **O– Overcome Early Attacks:** *Protecting minds and hearts.*
- ✓ **C – Cultivate Faith Early:** *Planting the seed of belief.*
- ✓ **U – Understand the Times:** *Preparing children for today's world.*
- ✓ **S – Send Them Out with Purpose:** *Empowering for destiny.*

Each of these principles forms a divine blueprint for raising powerful children—spiritually grounded, emotionally strong, and purpose-driven. The truths within these pages are drawn from Scripture, shaped by biblical examples, and brought to life through real-life stories of families, teachers, and mentors who dared to take their role seriously.

This is not a theoretical or theological book alone—it is a practical guide. You will find toolkits, prayers, declarations, and simple yet powerful activities that can be practiced at home, in classrooms, and in church settings. Whether you are a parent seeking to raise godly children, a teacher shaping young minds, a pastor nurturing the next generation, or simply someone who longs to make a difference—this book is for you.

God is a Builder (Hebrews 3:4), and He calls us to build with Him. Our assignment is not to merely manage the next generation but to mold them—to raise sons and daughters of purpose who carry the

fire of faith, integrity, and love for God into every sphere of life.
The task is urgent. The hour is late. But the promise remains sure—*"All your children shall be taught by the Lord, and great shall be the peace of your children."* (Isaiah 54:13)

So let us build together—with prayer as our foundation, love as our mortar, and the Word of God as our blueprint—believing that what we build today will echo through eternity.

The Battle for the Next Generation

Before a child takes their first breath, a battle is already being waged. It is not a battle of flesh and blood, but of spirits contending for destinies. The womb, meant to be a cradle of promise, has also become a battlefield of purpose. From the very beginning of human history, Satan has shown that his strategy is to start early — earlier than the Church, earlier than parents, earlier than we imagine.

The Spiritual War Over Children's Destinies

When God created humanity, He placed within every child a spark of divine purpose — a reflection of His image and potential to reveal His glory on earth (Genesis 1:27–28). But the enemy saw that purpose and declared war on it. From the garden of Eden to the present day, Satan's tactic has remained the same: corrupt the seed before it grows, confuse identity before it is formed, and crush destiny before it matures.

When Pharaoh saw that Israel was multiplying, his fear was not about the present — it was about the *future*. His command to drown every male child (Exodus 1:16, 22) was a demonic attempt to eliminate future deliverers. Yet, in that very generation, God preserved a baby named Moses, hidden in a basket by a river. Satan aimed to destroy, but God used the courage of a mother and the faith of a family to preserve a destiny that would one day deliver a nation.

In the New Testament, Herod repeated the same pattern. When the wise men spoke of a newborn King, he ordered the killing of all male infants in

Bethlehem (Matthew 2:16). The spirit of destruction once again sought to stop deliverance before it began. But divine intervention warned Joseph in a dream, leading to Jesus' protection in Egypt. From Moses to Jesus, we see that hell trembles when a child of destiny is born.

This is why Psalm 127:3–5 reminds us:

"Children are a heritage from the Lord, the fruit of the womb a reward. Like arrows in the hands of a warrior are children born in one's youth."

Every child is an arrow — but if not shaped, sharpened, and aimed rightly, that arrow may never reach its target. The question is: who is shaping the arrows — the world, the enemy, or the Kingdom?

Why Satan Starts Early — and Why the Church Must Respond Even Earlier

The enemy knows something the Church often forgets: habits and beliefs are easiest to shape when hearts are tender. Studies confirm what Scripture has already shown — that values and worldview are formed in the earliest years of life. That's why Satan aims for the cradle — because whoever captures the mind of a child, captures the direction of a nation.

In Eden, the serpent didn't attack Adam's strength; he went for Eve's perception. His goal wasn't just their fall — it was their offspring's future. In deceiving the first couple, the enemy planted corruption into the human race, tainting every generation thereafter. From that moment, the war for the seed began.

Fast-forward to today. The battlefield looks different — not a garden, but classrooms, screens, social media feeds, and entertainment. The serpent still whispers, but now through ideologies, confusion of identity, moral compromise, and spiritual apathy. The

strategy hasn't changed — just the medium. He still aims for the young.
But praise be to God — the Church is not called to react late, but to rise early. Deuteronomy 6:6–9 instructs parents:
"These commandments that I give you today are to be on your hearts. Impress them on your children. Talk about them when you sit at home, when you walk along the road, when you lie down and when you get up."
In other words, discipleship begins at home — not in Sunday school, but at the dining table, during bedtime, and in everyday moments. God designed families as the first faith training ground, not the church building.

The Family: God's First Training Ground of Faith
Before God established the Church, He established the family. The home was meant to be a mini-sanctuary — a place where faith is lived, taught, and modeled. The strength of the next generation depends not just on what children hear on Sundays, but on what they see from Monday to Saturday.
Consider Abraham. God didn't call him merely to be a father of nations, but first to be a father who instructs his household.
"For I have chosen him, so that he will direct his children and his household after him to keep the way of the LORD…" (Genesis 18:19)
When parents abdicate their spiritual roles, the enemy fills the vacuum. We cannot expect our children to walk in divine purpose if we outsource their discipleship to YouTube or television. Every Christian parent must become a pastor of their home

— shaping hearts, planting truth, and guarding minds.

Let's take a modern example.

Sarah, a devoted believer, worked tirelessly in ministry but rarely prayed with her 8-year-old son, Joel. She assumed he'd "catch up in Sunday school." One evening, she found Joel watching inappropriate content online. Her heart broke. Through tears, she realized that the devil had been discipling her son while she was busy serving God. She wept, repented, and began nightly prayer sessions with him. In months, she saw transformation — Joel started leading prayers at school and sharing Bible stories with friends.

That's how quickly the tide can turn when parents refocus on their divine assignment.

A Call to Parents, Teachers, and Leaders

The responsibility to raise godly children is not limited to parents alone. It extends to teachers, pastors, and anyone influencing young hearts. When Jesus welcomed the little children and rebuked His disciples for turning them away (Mark 10:13–16), He was showing us that children are not a distraction from ministry — they are the ministry.

We must stop treating children's ministry as a side department in the church. They are the *future apostles, prophets, evangelists, pastors, and teachers* (Ephesians 4:11).

If the enemy can pervert their calling early, the Kingdom will face a generational vacuum. But if the Church can disciple them early, the gates of hell will have no chance.

Old and New Testament Echoes

Samuel heard God's voice as a child (1 Samuel 3:4–10). Why? Because his mother Hannah had dedicated him early.

Josiah became king at eight and led a national revival at sixteen (2 Chronicles 34:1–3).

Timothy learned faith from his mother Eunice and grandmother Lois (2 Timothy 1:5). Paul later called him his "true son in the faith."

From these examples, we see that the earlier God's Word is sown, the greater the harvest.

Outcome: The Sacredness of Raising Children for God's Kingdom

If we could see what heaven sees, we would realize that every child is a potential history maker — a Moses, a Deborah, a Daniel, a Mary, a Timothy. The question is: who will shape them? If the Church delays, the world won't.

This book is a wake-up call to every believer — a call to reclaim the next generation. The enemy is not waiting for them to grow up before he starts his work; therefore, we cannot wait until they grow up to start ours.

It's time to fight for our children — not with fear, but with faith; not with anxiety, but with authority; not with reaction, but with revelation. The future of the Kingdom depends on it.

Prayer of Decree and Declaration

Heavenly Father,

We thank You for entrusting us with the greatest treasures of Your Kingdom — our children. Today, we stand as guardians of destiny, declaring that the next generation belongs to You.

We decree that no weapon formed against their minds, hearts, or purpose shall prosper *(Isaiah 54:17).*

We declare that they will grow in wisdom, stature, and favor with God and man *(Luke 2:52).*

We break every early assignment of the enemy over their lives and declare that from the womb to their destiny, Your hand shall guide them *(Psalm 139:13–16).*

Raise up parents, teachers, and leaders who will disciple children in truth and power.

Let our homes become altars, and our children become arrows in Your hand.

In Jesus' mighty name, we pray — Amen.

F – Formative Years Matter: Building from the Foundation Up

Key Verse: *"For You created my inmost being; You knit me together in my mother's womb. I praise You because I am fearfully and wonderfully made."* — Psalm 139:13–14

Every building that stands the test of time has one thing in common — a solid foundation. No architect, however skilled, can erect a lasting structure on a weak base. The same is true for a child's life. The earliest years — from the womb through early childhood — are the foundation stones upon which everything else is built. What a child hears, sees, and experiences during these tender years silently shapes the architecture of his or her soul.

When God formed a child in the womb, He did not merely create a biological being; He breathed purpose and destiny into that little one. The psalmist David marveled at this mystery when he said, *"You saw my unformed body; all the days ordained for me were written in Your book before one of them came to be"* (Psalm 139:16). Before a child ever takes a breath, God has already spoken destiny over their life. But Satan knows this too — and that is why he wages war so early.

The Womb: God's Creative Workshop

Science tells us that even in the womb, a child can hear sounds, feel emotions, and respond to their environment. But long before modern research confirmed it, Scripture had already declared it. When Elizabeth heard Mary's greeting, *"the baby leaped in her womb"* (Luke 1:41). That baby — John the

Baptist — responded to the presence of Jesus even before birth. What a powerful picture of divine sensitivity in the womb!

It tells us that spiritual life begins before physical life ever steps into the world. A mother's prayers, the words spoken over her unborn child, and the atmosphere in the home can shape the spiritual tone of that child's life. Satan, on the other hand, seeks to introduce fear, rejection, and confusion — even before the baby is born. How many expectant mothers wrestle with anxiety, depression, or conflict during pregnancy without realizing there's more at stake than emotion — it's a battle over what's forming inside?

When Jochebed gave birth to Moses during Pharaoh's cruel decree to kill every male Hebrew child (Exodus 1:22–2:10), she refused to surrender to fear. Her faith created a spiritual covering. While others obeyed Pharaoh, she hid her son, trusting that God had a greater plan. The child that she nursed and nurtured during those few early years would later stand before kings. Moses' courage and faith were not accidents of adulthood — they were the echoes of his mother's faith during his formative years.

The Power of Early Impressions

Children are like wet cement — whatever falls on them makes an impression. During the first few years of life, their hearts are incredibly receptive. They absorb not just what is said, but what is lived before them. Parents may not realize it, but every word spoken, every tone used, every argument or act of kindness — is a brushstroke painting their child's worldview.

Deuteronomy 6:6–9 instructs parents, *"These commandments that I give you today are to be upon your hearts. Impress them on your children. Talk about them when you sit at home, when you walk along the road, when you lie down and when you get up."* Notice the word *"impress."* Teaching faith is not about occasional sermons at home; it's about daily impressions through life's rhythms — breakfast conversations, bedtime prayers, shared worship moments, and even the way parents handle problems.

A father named Ruth (yes, an unusual but real name in this story) and his wife Daniela understood this truth after attending a family retreat. They realized that while they were committed believers, they had outsourced their children's spiritual growth to Sunday school. They decided to start a *"family altar time"* every morning. It was simple — ten minutes of a Bible story, a song, and prayer before the children left for school. Within months, the transformation was evident. Their once impatient son began praying for his classmates. Their little daughter, who struggled with fear at night, started singing worship songs before bed. The atmosphere in the home shifted — not by a grand miracle, but by the quiet consistency of godly impressions made in the formative years.

Identity and Values: The Hidden Roots

Children begin forming identity far earlier than most realize. Before they can spell their name, they are already answering the silent question: *"Who am I?"* This is where parents and guardians become the first prophets in a child's life. What you declare over your children will often determine what they believe about themselves. Godly words plant godly roots.

In the Old Testament, Hannah provides a beautiful example. Though she had longed for a child, when Samuel was finally born, she dedicated him to the Lord (1 Samuel 1:27–28). Her decision wasn't just a religious ritual — it was a declaration of ownership. She was saying, *"This child belongs to God, and his destiny will align with heaven's purpose."* As a result, Samuel grew into one of Israel's greatest prophets — a man who could hear God clearly in a corrupt generation. The foundation of that prophetic calling was laid not in Eli's temple, but in Hannah's home.

Parents today often underestimate the power of those formative declarations. When a child is constantly told, "You're stubborn," "You're careless," or "You'll never learn," those words carve deep grooves in their identity. But when they hear, "You're chosen," "You're wise," "You belong to Jesus," it builds resilience and faith. What we sow in their hearts becomes the fruit they live by tomorrow.

Creating a God-Centered Environment

A godly home isn't just one that has Bibles on shelves or Christian music playing in the background. It's an atmosphere saturated with love, peace, and presence. It's where forgiveness flows freely, where worship is not reserved for Sunday mornings, and where Scripture is not a rulebook but a lifestyle.

Every home has a "spirit" that dominates it. Some homes are heavy with anger and fear, others with laughter and grace. When a home carries the fragrance of Christ, children grow up associating faith with joy, not fear.

In the New Testament, we see this modeled in Timothy's life. Paul reminded him, *"I am reminded of your sincere faith, which first lived in your grandmother Lois and in your mother Eunice"* (2 Timothy 1:5). Long before Timothy became Paul's trusted co-laborer, he was shaped by the atmosphere of faith that surrounded him at home. His grandmother and mother didn't just teach him Scripture — they lived it. Faith in that house was contagious.

Practical Routines for a Godly Foundation

Parents often ask, "Where do we start?" The truth is, building spiritually strong children doesn't require grand gestures. It begins with small, consistent habits:

- ✓ **Start each day with prayer.** Even a two-minute family prayer invites God's presence before the day begins.
- ✓ **Tell Bible stories often.** Not as lifeless lessons, but as living truths that connect to your child's experiences.
- ✓ **Model forgiveness and gratitude.** Let your children see you pray when hurt, thank God when blessed, and apologize when wrong.
- ✓ **Worship together.** Sing, dance, and celebrate God's goodness — let joy be your family's sound of faith.

These habits become the spiritual DNA of your home. They don't just build well-behaved children; they raise warriors who know God personally.

Building Early, Building Strong

The formative years are sacred — they are the divine blueprint years. If Satan can distort identity early, he doesn't need to fight later; the damage is already done. But if parents, teachers, and mentors rise early

— to pray, teach, and love — we can raise a generation that walks in divine strength and wisdom. When the foundation is firm, the storms of life will come, but the house will stand. Jesus said, *"Everyone who hears these words of mine and puts them into practice is like a wise man who built his house on the rock"* (Matthew 7:24). Let's give our children that rock — firm, unshakable, and Christ-centered.

A Prayer of Decree

Father, *thank You for entrusting us with the precious lives of children.*

We decree that our homes shall be places where Your Spirit dwells, where truth and love are taught from the earliest days. We declare that no voice of the enemy shall steal their identity or purpose. From the womb, our children shall be marked for Your Kingdom. Their foundations shall be strong, their faith unshakable, and their futures secure in You.

In Jesus' name, Amen.

O – Overcome Early Attacks: Protecting Minds and Hearts

Key Verse: *"Be strong in the Lord and in the power of His might. Put on the full armor of God, so that you can take your stand against the devil's schemes."* — Ephesians 6:10–11

If Satan cannot destroy a life in the womb, his next target is the mind. The enemy understands a spiritual truth that many believers overlook — whoever wins the mind, wins the man. That's why he starts early. Long before a child can quote Scripture or understand doctrine, the battle for their thoughts and emotions has already begun.

Parents often imagine that their children's struggles — fears, temper tantrums, anxiety, or rebellion — are merely phases of growth. While some are indeed natural developments, many others have a spiritual root. The enemy doesn't wait until a child becomes an adult to begin his attack. He aims for the mind while it's still soft, the heart while it's still open, and the identity before it's fully formed.

Recognizing the Enemy's Early Tactics

The devil's weapons against children are rarely dramatic at first — they are subtle, quiet, and cunning. Fear becomes his favorite entry point. He plants nightmares that steal peace, whispers lies through media that distort truth, and manipulates peer influence to create insecurity. It's not by accident that even the youngest today know words like "anxiety," "depression," and "stress." The war over innocence has never been more aggressive.

In the Garden of Eden, Satan didn't attack Adam with a weapon — he used words. Deception, not destruction, was his opening move. He sowed doubt in Eve's mind by twisting God's truth: *"Did God really say…?"* (Genesis 3:1). That same strategy continues today. He whispers to children, *"You're not good enough." "You're not loved." "You can't trust God."* Once the seed of doubt is planted, it begins to shape how they see themselves and the world.

Modern culture, unfortunately, amplifies his voice. Through cartoons, songs, games, and even classroom ideologies, subtle messages of rebellion, confusion about identity, and disregard for holiness have become normalized. What once would shock now entertains. And many Christian parents, unaware, allow these seeds to grow unchecked.

The Authority of Parents and Teachers to Intercede

Yet, God has not left us defenseless. Parents, grandparents, teachers, and spiritual mentors are not passive observers — they are appointed gatekeepers. God has given them spiritual authority to intercede and guard the minds of their children.

When King Herod sought to kill the newborn Jesus, an angel appeared to Joseph in a dream, saying, *"Get up, take the child and his mother and escape to Egypt. Stay there until I tell you…"* (Matthew 2:13). Notice that divine protection required human obedience. God provided instruction, but Joseph had to act. He didn't question, delay, or negotiate. He rose immediately and protected the child from destruction.

That's how spiritual authority works in the family. Parents are the Josephs of this generation —

entrusted to hear from God and respond promptly. When the Spirit nudges a parent to pray, to monitor what a child watches, or to speak blessing, that's not a random feeling; it's a divine alert. Disobedience or delay can give the enemy ground, but swift obedience brings protection.

Breaking Generational Strongholds

Some attacks are not new; they are inherited. Generational strongholds — patterns of fear, addiction, anger, or failure — often run like invisible currents through family lines. Scripture shows this clearly. Abraham lied about his wife to protect himself (Genesis 12:13). Years later, his son Isaac repeated the same behavior (Genesis 26:7). What was tolerated in one generation was duplicated in the next.

But here's the good news — what began in the flesh can end in the Spirit. The curse may run through the bloodline, but the blood of Jesus runs stronger. Parents have the authority to break these chains through repentance and declaration.

I once met a couple — let's call them Michael and Anita — who came seeking prayer for their teenage son, whose constant anxiety and anger were crippling him. As we talked, Michael realized that he had battled the same torment in his youth, and his father before him had suffered similar mental distress. The family began nightly prayers, renouncing fear and declaring God's peace over their home. Within weeks, the atmosphere shifted. Their son began sleeping peacefully, and the constant tension in the house lifted. What counseling alone couldn't fix, spiritual authority restored.

Strongholds are like weeds — you don't just trim them; you uproot them. And it begins when parents take their stand not in frustration, but in faith.

Guarding Minds Through the Word

When Jesus was tempted in the wilderness, He didn't argue or debate with Satan — He spoke the Word. *"It is written..."* (Matthew 4:4). If that was the Son of God's strategy, it must be ours too. The Word of God is not a book of verses — it's a sword for battle.

Every time Scripture is spoken over a child, it builds what I call *spiritual immunity.* Just as vitamins strengthen the body against infection, the Word strengthens the soul against deception. When a child grows hearing, "You are fearfully and wonderfully made" (Psalm 139:14), it becomes harder for the world to convince them they're worthless. When they memorize, "God has not given us a spirit of fear" (2 Timothy 1:7), it arms them against anxiety.

One evening, John's parents noticed that their 8-year-old had been waking up in terror from recurring nightmares. He described seeing dark figures in his room and hearing whispers of fear. At first, they thought it was just imagination. But one night, sensing something spiritual, they decided to pray instead of pacify. They opened the Bible to Psalm 91, read it aloud, and declared God's protection over John. Then they taught him to say, "The Lord is my light and my salvation — whom shall I fear?" (Psalm 27:1) before bed each night. Within days, the nightmares stopped. The peace that settled in their home was undeniable. That family discovered what many forget — Scripture is not a bedtime story; it's a shield.

Spiritual Covering: The Invisible Hedge

Parents must remember: protection isn't only physical; it's spiritual. Job's life gives us a remarkable picture. The devil complained to God, *"Have You not put a hedge around him and his household and everything he has?"* (Job 1:10). That hedge didn't appear by accident — it was the result of Job's continual prayers and sacrifices for his children (Job 1:5). Every prayer a parent prays, every blessing spoken, every act of obedience builds that invisible hedge.

That is what "overcoming early attacks" means — not reacting in fear when darkness shows up, but building such a hedge of light that darkness cannot even approach.

Toolkit: Daily Prayer and Declarations for Children

Below is a sample you can adapt in your own words and use daily. It's not a formula but a faith-based framework — a way to keep the armor of God on your child's life.

Morning Prayer (Parent with Child):

"Father, I thank You for this precious life You've entrusted to me. Today, I cover my child with the blood of Jesus. I decree that no weapon formed against them shall prosper. I speak peace to their mind, purity to their thoughts, and purpose to their heart. Let Your Word be their shield and truth their compass. May they walk in wisdom, courage, and joy. In Jesus' name, amen."

Scripture Declarations:

"I am fearfully and wonderfully made." (Psalm 139:14)

"The Lord is my light and my salvation; whom shall I fear?" (Psalm 27:1)
"God has not given me a spirit of fear, but of power, love, and a sound mind." (2 Timothy 1:7)
"No weapon formed against me shall prosper." (Isaiah 54:17)
"Greater is He that is in me than he that is in the world." (1 John 4:4)

Bedtime Blessing (Parent over Child):

"May the Lord bless you and keep you. May His angels surround your dreams. May your heart rest in His peace and your thoughts be guarded by His Word. You belong to Jesus, and He watches over you always."

The Power of a Protected Mind

The greatest battles are fought not in the heavens, but in the hidden thoughts of young hearts. Every child is a battlefield of destiny — and the earlier we guard them, the stronger they grow. When parents and teachers rise in prayer and discernment, children are not only protected; they are prepared to face the world with strength and clarity.

Ephesians 6:13 reminds us, *"Therefore put on the full armor of God, so that when the day of evil comes, you may be able to stand your ground."* When we clothe our children daily with truth, righteousness, faith, salvation, and the Word of God, they are not merely surviving in a dark world — they are shining through it.

C – Cultivate Faith Early: Planting the Seed of Belief

Key Verse*: "And that from a child thou hast known the holy scriptures, which are able to make thee wise unto salvation through faith which is in Christ Jesus."*
– 2 Timothy 3:15 (KJV)

There is a tender window in every child's life when their heart is open, curious, and unpolluted by cynicism. This is the fertile soil where faith must be planted — not through strict rules or religious obligation, but through relationship, love, and trust in the living God. Faith does not start in the pews of a church; it begins in the atmosphere of the home, in the conversations around the table, in the bedtime stories whispered before sleep, and in the small prayers said over scraped knees and school tests.

Faith Begins with Relationship, Not Rules

When faith is presented as a list of dos and don'ts, children grow up knowing religion but not God. But when faith is introduced as a friendship with Jesus — a real, living Savior who listens, comforts, guides, and forgives — the child's spirit learns to lean on Him naturally. Rules may shape behavior for a season, but relationship transforms the heart for life.

In the Old Testament, we see this truth beautifully reflected in the life of Samuel, a child dedicated to God from birth. His mother, Hannah, had prayed for him earnestly, vowing to give him back to the Lord (1 Samuel 1:27–28). True to her word, she left Samuel under the care of Eli the priest at the temple. But though Samuel grew up in a religious environment, it wasn't ritual that defined his faith — it was a personal encounter. One night, as he lay down to sleep, he heard God call his name. "Samuel!" The young boy mistook the voice for Eli's until the old priest realized it was the Lord speaking. Eli wisely instructed him, "If He calls you again, say, 'Speak, Lord, for your servant is listening'" (1 Samuel 3:9).

This single act of obedience — of a child learning to listen and respond to God — became the foundation of Samuel's lifelong prophetic ministry. It reminds parents and teachers that cultivating faith is not about forcing knowledge into a child's head, but awakening their awareness of God's presence in their heart.

Teaching Children How to Pray, Hear God, and Trust Him

Prayer should never be introduced to children as a religious duty but as a conversation with their heavenly Father. When children realize they can talk to God anytime, anywhere — while walking to school, drawing, or falling asleep — faith becomes natural.

In the New Testament, Jesus Himself welcomed children, rebuking His disciples when they tried to keep them away. "Let the little children come to me," He said, "for the kingdom of heaven belongs to such as these" (Matthew 19:14). Jesus didn't require eloquent prayers or perfect behavior from them — He simply wanted their presence, their simplicity, their belief. That same openness is what parents must nurture.

Consider the story of Leah, a nine-year-old girl whose parents taught her to pray about everything. One day, her best friend Mia fell ill and was hospitalized with a severe infection. Instead of worrying, Leah decided to pray. She took a small card, wrote "Dear Jesus, please heal Mia," and kept it under her pillow. Every night, she prayed the same prayer with childlike confidence. A week later, Mia's condition improved dramatically, and she was discharged. When Leah heard the news, she smiled and said, "I knew Jesus would help her." That simple yet profound act of faith became a cornerstone for Leah's growing trust in God.

Such experiences, small as they seem, are the building blocks of lifelong faith. A parent's role is not to make children understand every theological concept, but to help them experience the reality of a God who listens, answers, and loves.

Using Storytelling, Testimonies, and Life Examples to Build Faith

Children's hearts respond powerfully to stories — and the Bible is full of them. From Noah's ark to David's victory over Goliath, from Daniel in the lions' den to the miracles of Jesus, each story reveals the character of a faithful God who delivers, protects, and provides. Parents and teachers should make storytelling a daily practice, weaving in testimonies of how God has worked in their own lives.

For example, a father might tell his children how God provided finances when their family faced a difficult time, or a mother might share how prayer brought peace in moments of fear. These real-life testimonies turn abstract faith into something tangible and personal.

In Deuteronomy 6:6–7, God commands parents, "These words that I command you today shall be on your heart. You shall teach them diligently to your children, and shall talk of them when you sit in your house, when you walk by the way, and when you lie down, and when you rise." This scripture paints a picture of continuous conversation — faith that flows through daily life rather than being confined to Sunday sermons.

Helping Children See God's Hand in Daily Life

Faith grows when children learn to connect God with the ordinary. When they find a lost toy after praying, or when the rain stops just in time for a school event, they begin to see that God is not distant but involved in their everyday world. Parents can help by naming these moments: "See, God answered your prayer," or "That was God's protection."

This practice awakens spiritual awareness — the ability to recognize divine fingerprints in the routine. It teaches gratitude, humility, and dependence on God rather than luck or coincidence. Over time, this awareness forms a habit of thanksgiving that anchors a child's heart in faith.

Encouraging Gratitude, Repentance, and Forgiveness Early

Faith flourishes in an atmosphere of grace. Teaching children early to say "thank you," "I'm sorry," and "I forgive you" are not just manners — they are spiritual disciplines that mirror the heart of God. Gratitude opens the door to joy; repentance keeps the heart soft and humble; forgiveness frees the spirit from bitterness.

When a child learns to forgive a friend who hurt them or to thank God for a small blessing, they are already practicing faith in action. In Luke 17:15–19, only one of ten healed lepers returned to thank Jesus, and that man received more than healing — he received wholeness. Teaching children gratitude early ensures they grow into believers who not only seek God's hand but cherish His heart.

Practical Tools: "Faith Moments" — Family Activities to Cultivate Childlike Faith

Faith Jar: Keep a jar where every family member writes down answered prayers or moments where they saw God's hand at work. Read them together every month as a reminder of God's faithfulness.

Story Sundays: Once a week, pick a Bible story and re-enact it as a family. Let children play roles — David, Moses, or Esther — so they experience faith in motion.

Thankful Tree: Create a small "tree" from twigs in a vase and hang paper leaves on it, each leaf representing something the family is thankful for that week.

Listening Time: Teach children to sit quietly after prayer and ask, "Lord, is there something You want to tell me today?" Then encourage them to share what they sense.

Cultivating faith early is not about producing perfect children — it's about planting seeds that will bear fruit in time. Like Samuel, like Leah, children who learn to recognize God's voice and trust His heart will stand firm in a wavering world. As 2 Timothy 3:15 reminds us, it is the Word of God that makes even a child wise unto salvation.

So, start early. Pray together. Tell stories. Celebrate God's goodness. Let faith be caught, not just taught. For the faith you plant today in your child's heart will one day grow into the tree that shelters generations to come.

Faith Moments Toolkit

Accompanying previous Chapter:
"Cultivate Faith Early: Planting the Seed of Belief"

This toolkit can be printed and used by parents, teachers, or faith mentors to make family faith-building moments simple, memorable, and deeply spiritual.
Everything is written in a warm, natural, and human tone — as though from one believing parent to another.

---

1. FAITH JAR — "Record His Faithfulness"
Purpose:
To help children see how God answers prayers and acts in daily life.
You'll Need:

- ✓ A jar, box, or container (can decorate with "God's Faithfulness Jar")
- ✓ Small paper slips or cards
- ✓ Pen or pencil

How to Use:
Every time a prayer is answered, or something special happens that reminds the family of God's goodness, write it down on a slip of paper.
Example:

- ✓ "God helped me not to be afraid at my school play." – Sarah, Age 7
- ✓ "Dad's project got approved after we prayed together."

Drop it into the jar.
Once a month (or every Sunday evening), open the jar together and read the slips aloud.
End by saying together:

"Thank You, Lord, for being faithful. Your goodness never fails."

Printable Slip Template:

FAITH JAR RECORD

Date: ____________________________________

What God did for us: ________________________

How I felt: _______________________________

Thank You, Lord, for: ______________________

Suggested Verse to Paste on the Jar:

"I will remember the deeds of the Lord; yes, I will remember your miracles of long ago." – Psalm 77:11

---

2. THANKFUL TREE — "Gratitude Grows Faith"

Purpose:

To cultivate a spirit of gratitude and joy in children.

You'll Need:

- ✓ A small branch or twig placed in a vase
- ✓ Colored paper cut into leaf shapes (or print leaf templates below)
- ✓ String or tape to hang them

How to Use:

- ✓ Every evening or week, ask: "What are we thankful for this week?"
- ✓ Write one item per leaf.
- ✓ Hang the leaves on the tree as a visible reminder of God's blessings.
- ✓ Once a month, pray together thanking God for every leaf.

Printable Leaf Template:

THANKFUL TREE LEAF

Today, I thank God for:

____

Because:

____

Date: ______________ Name: ___________________

Suggested Verse:
"Give thanks in all circumstances; for this is the will of God in Christ Jesus for you." – 1 Thessalonians 5:18

---

3. STORY SUNDAYS — "Faith Comes by Hearing"

Purpose:

To use Bible stories and real-life testimonies to build belief and connect faith to daily life.

You'll Need:

- ✓ A Bible
- ✓ Simple props (blanket for robe, paper crown, cardboard sword, etc.)
- ✓ A short space of 15–20 minutes every Sunday

How to Use:

Pick a story (e.g., David & Goliath, Daniel in the lions' den, Jesus calming the storm).

Read it aloud together or act it out with children playing parts.

End by asking:

- ✓ *"What did this story show us about God?"*
- ✓ *"What can we do like the hero in the story?"*

Close with a short prayer:

"Lord, help us to trust You like David did."

Printable Story Card Template:

STORY SUNDAY RECORD

Story Title: ________________________________

Bible Reference: ____________________________

What I learned about God: ____________________

What I can do this week: ______________________

Suggested Verse:
"So then faith comes by hearing, and hearing by the word of God." – Romans 10:17

---

4. LISTENING TIME — "Speak, Lord, Your Servant is Listening"

Purpose:
To teach children to hear God's voice in stillness and sensitivity.

You'll Need:
- ✓ A quiet moment (morning or bedtime)
- ✓ A notebook or "Listening Journal"

How to Use:
Begin with a short prayer:
"Lord Jesus, I love You. Please speak to my heart today."
Sit quietly for a minute or two.
Ask your child: *"Did you feel anything? Hear a thought or see a picture?"*
Write down what they sensed — even if it's simple ("Jesus loves me," "Don't be afraid," "Help others").
Over time, they will grow confident in recognizing God's gentle voice.

Printable Journal Template:
LISTENING JOURNAL
Date: ____
What I felt/heard God say: __________________________
What I will do about it: ____________________________
Thank You, Lord, for speaking to me.

Suggested Verse:
"My sheep listen to my voice; I know them, and they follow me." – John 10:27

---

5. FAMILY PRAYER PROMPTS — "Faith at Home"

Purpose:

To help families pray together intentionally each day.

How to Use:

Print and cut out the following Prayer Prompts Cards. Place them in a bowl or box. Each day, pick one card to pray together.

Printable Prayer Prompt Cards:

PRAYER PROMPT CARD 1

Thank You, Lord, for our family.
Help us love one another like You love us.

PRAYER PROMPT CARD 2

Lord Jesus, help me to be kind to my friends today.
Let me show Your light through my actions.

PRAYER PROMPT CARD 3

Heavenly Father, protect us today.
Keep us safe in school, work, and play.

PRAYER PROMPT CARD 4

Lord, help me forgive quickly and say sorry when I'm wrong.
Teach me to have a soft heart.

PRAYER PROMPT CARD 5

Thank You, Lord, for all our blessings.
Help us share what we have with those in need.

Suggested Verse for Family Prayer Time:

"The prayer of a righteous person is powerful and effective." – James 5:16

6. MEMORY VERSE CARDS — "Hide His Word in Our Hearts"

Purpose:

To help children memorize and meditate on short scriptures that build faith.

How to Use:

Print the following cards, cut them out, and place one each week on the fridge, study desk, or mirror.

Printable Scripture Cards:

WEEK 1

"The Lord is my shepherd; I lack nothing." – Psalm 23:1

WEEK 2

"I can do all things through Christ who strengthens me." – Philippians 4:13

WEEK 3

"When I am afraid, I put my trust in You." – Psalm 56:3

WEEK 4

"With God all things are possible." – Matthew 19:26

WEEK 5

"Give thanks to the Lord, for He is good." – Psalm 107:1

---

7. FAMILY BLESSING DECLARATION — "Speaking Life Over Our Home"

Purpose:

To close each day or week with spoken blessings that build a positive spiritual atmosphere.

Printable Declaration:

"Father, we thank You for our home.
We declare that Jesus is Lord over this family.
Our hearts are filled with faith, peace, and love.
We will trust You in every situation.
We are blessed coming in and blessed going out.
We choose to walk in Your ways, and our children will grow strong in faith, filled with wisdom and favor.
In Jesus' name, Amen."

Scripture Reference:

"The Lord bless you and keep you; the Lord make his face shine upon you and be gracious to you." – Numbers 6:24–25

CLOSING NOTE

Faith is not caught in a single moment — it's built through daily rhythms of remembrance, gratitude, and trust.

Every *Faith Moment* in this toolkit is a seed. Some will sprout quickly; others will take time. But as families keep sowing in love and consistency, they will one day look back and see a beautiful garden of faith flourishing in their home.

U – Understand the Times: Preparing Children for Today's World

Key Verse: *"From the tribe of Issachar, men who understood the times and knew what Israel should do."* — 1 Chronicles 12:32

There has never been a time in history when childhood has been so invaded, influenced, and interrupted as it is today. From the moment a child opens their eyes, they are surrounded by screens, voices, and images all competing for their attention — and, more dangerously, their allegiance. In the past, children learned values through stories told at the family table, through shared worship, and through the consistent example of godly parents. But now, technology, media, and modern ideologies are shaping young minds at lightning speed — faster than the Church is responding.

To "understand the times" as parents, mentors, and spiritual leaders means to discern what is shaping this generation and to prepare our children to stand in truth amidst confusion. The same spirit of discernment that guided the sons of Issachar is desperately needed today. They were not simply aware of the events unfolding around them — they *understood* them through the lens of God's purpose. They were spiritually alert, culturally aware, and morally grounded — qualities every believing parent should cultivate in their children.

Recognizing the Battle for the Mind

The Apostle Paul's warning in *Romans 12:2* is more relevant now than ever:

"Do not conform to the pattern of this world, but be transformed by the renewing of your mind."

The "pattern of this world" today comes disguised as entertainment, opinion, and convenience. Children are being taught — sometimes subtly, sometimes overtly — that truth is relative, that self is supreme, and that morality is optional. Even cartoons and social media platforms preach ideologies that conflict with God's Word. When left unguarded, these patterns mold how a child perceives right and wrong, love and identity, purpose and pleasure.

The enemy doesn't attack with horns and fire — he whispers through trends, normalizes through repetition, and numbs through distraction. Just as Herod sought to destroy the Christ-child early, today's cultural forces seek to destroy *Christ-likeness* early.

That is why parents must wake up with discernment — not in fear, but in faith and vigilance.

Teaching Discernment in a Digital Age

Discernment is not suspicion — it is spiritual perception guided by truth. It is the ability to separate the holy from the harmful, the temporary from the eternal. Teaching children discernment means helping them ask the right questions:

- ✓ *Is this pleasing to God?*
- ✓ *Does this draw me closer to Him or away from Him?*
- ✓ *What does the Word of God say about this?*

In today's world, those questions must extend to movies, YouTube videos, social media trends, and even friendships. Children must learn that not everything popular is right — and not everything right will be popular.

In the Old Testament, we find Daniel, a young teenager taken to Babylon — a culture filled with idolatry, luxury, and moral compromise. Yet Daniel "resolved not to defile himself" (Daniel 1:8). He discerned the spirit of Babylon and made a stand, even when surrounded by those who didn't share his convictions. His courage and clarity came not from isolation, but from internal conviction — a faith so deeply rooted that no cultural pressure could sway him.

That same strength is what our children need today — conviction shaped by God's Word, not by public opinion.

Building Resilience Against Confusion and Anxiety

Children today face pressures that previous generations never did — identity confusion, social comparison, academic stress, and digital overstimulation. These pressures have created what experts call a *crisis of self-worth*. But long before psychology defined it, Scripture already provided the cure: *identity in Christ.*

When children know who they are in God, they become resilient against confusion and anxiety. Ephesians 2:10 says,

"For we are His workmanship, created in Christ Jesus for good works."

Parents must consistently affirm identity with Scripture, not with worldly success. When a child knows, *"I am loved by God, chosen, and made with purpose,"* no trend, comment, or comparison can easily shake them.

Real-Life Example: Anna's Prayer Club

David and Rebecca were parents who understood that their teenage daughter Anna was growing up in a culture that challenged faith at every turn. When Anna entered high school, she encountered ridicule for believing in God. Instead of retreating, she prayed for courage. One day, during her lunch break, she invited two friends to pray with her for the school, their teachers, and their classmates.

They called it "Light Lunch" — fifteen minutes of prayer and reading one Psalm before the next class. Word spread. By the end of the year, there were fifteen students meeting twice a week. Anna told her parents one evening, "I used to be scared to speak up, but when I started praying with others, I felt stronger inside."

David later said, "We realized our job wasn't to protect her from the world but to prepare her to shine in it."

That's what understanding the times looks like — raising children who discern the culture yet stand courageously within it.

Equipping Children with a Biblical Worldview

Every child will one day have to answer questions about morality, purpose, gender, faith, and truth. If the Church and parents do not prepare them, the world will. A biblical worldview is not just head knowledge; it's seeing the world through God's eyes.

When a child learns early that God is Creator, that truth is absolute, and that love and obedience walk hand in hand, they grow with moral clarity. The Bible

must not be treated as an occasional reading but as a living lens through which life is understood.
Parents can create worldview moments daily:

- ✓ *When watching a movie, ask, "What message did that story teach?"*
- ✓ *When facing a problem, ask, "What does the Bible say about this?"*
- ✓ *When a news story shocks or saddens, ask, "How can we pray for this situation?"*

Through these conversations, the home becomes the training ground of discernment.

Biblical Example: The Sons of Issachar
The sons of Issachar in 1 Chronicles 12:32 were few in number, yet their influence was remarkable because they *"understood the times and knew what Israel should do."*
They had spiritual intelligence — the ability to interpret current events in light of divine purpose. While others reacted to what was happening, Issachar responded to what God was saying.
In every generation, God raises "Issachars" — parents, mentors, and teachers who read the spiritual climate and prepare the next generation to navigate it. Understanding the times is not about predicting trends; it's about perceiving truth amidst them.

Practical Parental Guidelines: Digital Discernment and Godly Worldview
Set Digital Boundaries:
Devices should not dominate family time. Establish tech-free zones — especially during meals, devotion time, and bedtime. Teach children that screens are tools, not masters.
Curate What Enters the Home:

Just as Nehemiah guarded the city gates, parents must guard the "gates" of the home — the eyes, ears, and hearts of children. Review media content and discuss why certain things are avoided, not just banned.

Pray Over Every Device:

Dedicate your child's phone, tablet, or computer to God. Pray aloud, "Lord, let these be tools for learning, creating, and glorifying You — not for distraction or deception."

Equip with the Word:

Encourage Scripture memorization tied to daily challenges. If your child fears rejection, teach Romans 8:31. If they struggle with identity, declare Psalm 139:14. The Word renews the mind.

Model Discernment Yourself:

Children learn discernment not just by instruction but by observation. Let them see you pause before reacting, pray before deciding, and evaluate everything through God's truth.

New Testament Example: Jesus Among the Teachers

In Luke 2:46–47, we read of young Jesus sitting among the teachers in the temple, listening and asking questions. Though still a child, He was spiritually alert, intellectually curious, and scripturally grounded. This moment shows that understanding the times begins with *understanding God's truth early.*

Jesus didn't withdraw from culture — He engaged it with wisdom. He grew "in wisdom and stature, and in favor with God and man" (Luke 2:52). That must be our goal for every child — not isolation from the world, but illumination within it.

A Call to Parents and Mentors

Understanding the times doesn't mean living in fear of the world; it means preparing our children to influence it. When they know who they are in Christ, they won't need to chase approval or follow every trend.

Let us raise children who are aware but not anxious, informed but not influenced, surrounded by culture but shaped by Christ. As Jesus prayed in John 17:15–18,

"I do not ask that You take them out of the world, but that You keep them from the evil one."

That is the parent's prayer and mission — not escape, but empowerment.

Closing Reflection

Every generation faces its test. Ours is the digital flood, the storm of information, and the moral drift of society. But God has not left us unequipped. He gives wisdom to those who seek it, and He calls families to stand as beacons of light.

Let your home be a sanctuary of truth in a world of confusion. Let your children grow as Daniels and Esthers — wise, bold, and discerning. And may God raise in this generation a new tribe of Issachars — children who understand the times and know what their God is calling them to do.

S – Send Them Out with Purpose: Empowering for Destiny

There comes a moment in every parent's journey when the hands that once held a child tightly must learn to release. This releasing is not abandonment—it is empowerment. To "send them out with purpose" means to raise children who know *why* they are here, *who* sent them, and *what* God has placed within them. It is about preparing them not merely for success in the world but for significance in the Kingdom.

Every child born on earth carries a divine assignment. Before their first cry was heard, Heaven had already whispered their name into destiny's book. God told Jeremiah, *"Before I formed you in the womb I knew you, before you were born I set you apart; I appointed you as a prophet to the nations"* (Jeremiah 1:5). These are not poetic words for one prophet alone; they echo a truth for every generation—that each life is *intentional*, crafted with purpose, and called to shine.

Recognizing the Calling Within

The early years of a child's life are filled with small glimpses of divine design—how a child loves to organize, create, sing, lead, or comfort others. These are not random traits; they are seeds of calling. Parents who pay attention to these seeds can begin watering them through encouragement, prayer, and opportunities to serve.

In the Old Testament, we see Hannah doing this beautifully with her son Samuel. She didn't just dedicate him to God in a ceremony—she *released* him into divine service. When he was old enough, she brought him to Eli, saying, *"I prayed for this child, and the Lord has granted me what I asked of Him. So now I give him to the Lord. For his whole life he will be given over to the Lord"* (1 Samuel 1:27–28). Hannah's heart must have trembled as she let go, but her release became Samuel's destiny. Her son grew up to hear God's voice and shape the spiritual direction of a nation.

In today's world, releasing a child might not mean sending them to a temple, but it could mean letting them step into places where God can use them—youth groups, school projects, community service, music teams, or even missions. What matters is that parents and mentors do not *hold back* out of fear but *send forth* in faith.

Building Confidence and Courage

Modern culture often fills children with doubt about their worth or ability. They are told to compare, to perform, to seek validation from social media likes rather than divine affirmation. But God never sends His children out timidly. The Apostle Paul reminded young Timothy, *"For God has not given us a spirit of fear, but of power and love and a sound mind"* (2 Timothy 1:7). When children are rooted in identity, they can step out boldly.

Let's take an example from a modern family. David and Miriam had a 15-year-old son named Caleb. From a young age, Caleb loved music—he would sit for hours humming melodies, filling the house with worship songs. His parents noticed how music drew him closer to God, so they nurtured it by enrolling him in the church's youth worship team. When Caleb expressed fear about leading worship, his father prayed over him, anointing his hands and declaring, “You will play and lead for the glory of God, not for applause.”

Months later, Caleb was asked to lead worship at his school’s Christian fellowship. Nervous but prayerful, he accepted. The morning he stood before his classmates, his heart raced—but as he began to sing, peace filled the room. That small act of obedience became a ripple. Other students began to join, and soon a weekly worship time began in their school auditorium. Caleb’s parents didn’t push him into destiny—they *released* him into it.

Teaching Leadership, Service, and Responsibility

Children discover their true calling when they serve. Jesus taught His disciples that *“whoever wants to become great among you must be your servant”* (Matthew 20:26). In the New Testament, we see how Jesus sent out His followers two by two (Mark 6:7). He didn’t keep them under constant supervision but entrusted them to go, heal, preach, and act in His authority. That same principle applies to children—teach them early that leadership is not about titles, but about *service*.

In one local church, Pastor Ruth started a “Kingdom Builders” club for kids aged 10 to 14. Each child had a weekly responsibility—some visited the elderly, others collected food for those in need, while a few led short prayers during family devotions. One boy, Aaron, initially shy and withdrawn, was asked to deliver groceries to a struggling neighbor. Over time, he began praying with those families. His confidence grew, not because someone taught him leadership, but because he *experienced* it through service.

Parents who give children small responsibilities—praying before meals, helping siblings, reading Scripture aloud—are not just teaching discipline; they're nurturing destiny.

Releasing with Confidence, Not Fear

Releasing children into their God-ordained purpose can be one of the hardest acts of faith. It means trusting that the God who called them will guide them. Moses' mother, Jochebed, faced this moment when she placed her baby into a basket and set him afloat on the Nile (Exodus 2:3). That basket was her act of surrender. Yet, God honored it—Pharaoh's daughter found Moses, and his destiny as a deliverer began to unfold. Jochebed didn't lose her son; she positioned him for purpose.

Likewise, when parents pray and release their children, they hand them into the safest hands possible—God's.

Commissioning with Blessing and Prophecy

The final act of sending must be spiritual. Words have creative power. When parents and mentors *speak blessing*, they plant destiny. Before Jesus ascended, He lifted His hands and *blessed* His disciples (Luke 24:50). That blessing wasn't just farewell—it was empowerment.

Families today can reclaim this tradition. Gather your children, lay hands on them, and declare God's promises over their lives. A simple prophetic commissioning might sound like this:

"You are a light set on a hill. You will walk in truth and courage. You will fulfill every purpose for which God created you. No fear, no confusion, no

compromise will take you off course. The Lord bless you, protect you, and establish you in His will."
These moments shape identity far more than lectures ever can.

Purpose Discovery Guide
A Practical Toolkit for Parents and Mentors
The following guide is designed as a simple, ready-to-use resource that families can print and fill out together. It helps children begin recognizing their God-given gifts and sense of calling.
1. Discovering the Gifts Within
Step 1 – Observation Journal:
- ✓ *Parents and children each keep a small notebook for two weeks.*
- ✓ *Parents note: "What brings my child joy? What do they do naturally well?"*

Children note: *"What do I love doing most? When do I feel closest to God?"*
At the end, compare notes. Discuss similarities—it's often where calling begins.
Step 2 – Gift Clusters:
Help your child identify if their gifts fall under any of these areas:
- ✓ **Creative Gifts** (art, music, writing)
- ✓ **Compassion Gifts** (caring, helping others)
- ✓ **Leadership Gifts** (organizing, guiding)

Wisdom Gifts (teaching, problem-solving)
Then read Romans 12:6–8 together and pray:
"Lord, show us how to use these gifts for Your glory."

---

2. Purpose Prayer Card
Create a small index card your child can keep in their Bible or bag:

Front:
"My life has purpose because God made me for His glory."
Back:
"Lord, help me use my gifts to serve You and others. Guide my steps and give me courage to live for You each day."
Encourage them to say this daily before school.

---

3. Family Commissioning Ceremony
Once a year, gather as a family. Light a candle to represent God's guidance. Each parent or guardian speaks a short blessing over the child's life, such as:
"We bless you to be a truth-bearer, a light in darkness, a vessel of peace."
Then, pray together:
"Lord, we release this child into Your perfect plan. Lead them, protect them, and make them fruitful in Your Kingdom."
End by reading Matthew 5:14–16 aloud:
"You are the light of the world. A city set on a hill cannot be hidden."
Let this be the banner over their life.

Final Thought
To *send them out with purpose* is not merely to say goodbye—it is to say *go with God*. It is the culmination of faith-filled parenting: sowing, nurturing, and finally releasing what belongs to the Lord. When children step out, carrying the light of Christ within, parents can rest knowing they have done their part in Heaven's great story.

Raising a Spiritual Atmosphere in the Home

Key Verse: Joshua 24:15 — *"As for me and my house, we will serve the Lord."*

Every home carries an atmosphere. Sometimes it's filled with peace and laughter, other times with tension and silence. But beyond the emotions and moods that drift through our walls, there is a spiritual atmosphere that defines a home — one that either welcomes the presence of God or allows confusion, strife, and fear to settle in.

A Christian home is meant to be far more than a shelter or a place of comfort. It is meant to be a *sanctuary*, a *mini-church*, where hearts are nurtured, faith is lived out daily, and God's presence is made real to every member. When Joshua boldly declared, *"As for me and my house, we will serve the Lord,"* he wasn't making a slogan for his wall; he was making a covenant. He was saying, "This home belongs to God — everything that happens here must reflect His rule."

The Home as a Mini-Church

The early church didn't begin in cathedrals or temples; it began in homes. The book of Acts tells us that *"they broke bread in their homes and ate together with glad and sincere hearts, praising God"* (Acts 2:46–47). Homes were the first churches, where teaching, worship, and prayer flowed naturally through family life.

In many Christian households today, the home has become a place of busyness rather than blessing. Meals are rushed, conversations are shallow, and the glow of screens has replaced the warmth of prayer. Yet, the moment parents decide to invite God back into the center, everything changes. The dining table becomes an altar of thanksgiving. Bedrooms become places of prayer. Hallways echo with songs of praise.

In the New Testament, we see a beautiful example in the life of Lois and Eunice, Timothy's grandmother and mother. Paul writes, *"I am reminded of your sincere faith, which first lived in your grandmother Lois and in your mother Eunice and, I am persuaded, now lives in you also"* (2 Timothy 1:5). Their home was clearly a place where faith was taught and lived out daily. There's no record of grand miracles or dramatic sermons—just the quiet, consistent faith of two women who turned their household into holy ground.

Timothy's faith was not born in a church building—it was *cultivated at home*.

The Power of Godly Communication, Worship, and Conflict Resolution

Words shape the spiritual climate of a home. Proverbs 18:21 says, *"Death and life are in the power of the tongue."* When parents speak harshly or critically, they unknowingly sow fear and insecurity into their children's hearts. But when they speak life, encouragement, and blessing, they create a spiritual atmosphere where faith thrives.

Consider the story of Peter and Naomi, a young couple with two children, Aaron (10) and Grace (7). Their home was often filled with tension — arguments over finances, chores, and discipline. The children began to mirror that same spirit at school, becoming anxious and argumentative. One evening after a particularly harsh exchange, Naomi wept before God, realizing their home's atmosphere was affecting their children's peace.

Together, Peter and Naomi decided to change course. They began to pray together every morning before their children woke up. They made a new rule: no argument would end without prayer. Instead of harsh words, they chose soft answers. Within weeks, laughter began to return to their home. Aaron started waking up singing songs from church, and Grace began praying before meals voluntarily.

That transformation wasn't magic—it was atmosphere. They didn't change their home's furniture; they changed its *spirit*.

When families worship together, read Scripture aloud, and resolve conflict in love, they invite the Holy Spirit to dwell richly among them. The home becomes a safe place again—a training ground for heaven.

Establishing Family Devotions that Engage Children's Hearts

Family devotions shouldn't feel like a chore; they should feel like a conversation with God. Many parents make the mistake of turning devotion time into a lecture. Children disengage because it feels like school, not relationship. The goal is not to complete a reading—it's to connect hearts.

Here's how to make devotions come alive:

Begin with simple worship—one or two songs that everyone can join in. Then, read a short passage and ask open-ended questions like, "What do you think this means?" or "How can we live this today?" Close with prayer, allowing each member to share one thing they're thankful for and one person they'd like to pray for.

In the Old Testament, God instructed Israel, *"These commandments that I give you today are to be on your hearts. Impress them on your children. Talk about them when you sit at home and when you walk along the road"* (Deuteronomy 6:6–7). Notice how faith was never meant to be confined to one time slot—it was to *flow naturally through life*.

A family that worships together doesn't need a perfect structure; they just need *consistency and sincerity*. Even ten minutes a day can shift the spiritual tone of an entire household.

Breaking the Spirit of Division, Fear, and Apathy in Homes

The enemy's oldest strategy has always been *division*. From Adam and Eve's blame-shifting in Eden to Cain's resentment toward Abel, Satan understands that where unity breaks, power drains. Jesus Himself said, *"A house divided against itself cannot stand"* (Mark 3:25).

Many Christian homes are not under attack because of what they do wrong, but because of what they fail to do—pray together. Silence between spouses, coldness between parents and children, or unspoken offenses create cracks where darkness seeps in.

Daniel and Ruth, parents of three teenage boys, once faced such division. Each son was consumed with screens, rarely joining family meals. Daniel, often exhausted from work, stayed glued to his phone, while Ruth retreated to online devotionals in isolation. The house was quiet—but spiritually empty. One night, after a heated argument over discipline, Daniel sensed the Holy Spirit prompting him to "take

back the home." The next morning, he gathered the family and confessed, "We've let the world shape our habits. But from today, our home belongs to God again." They began a new routine: dinner without devices, nightly prayer, and worship on Sundays together. Slowly, their home began to breathe again.
The fear that once gripped them began to fade. The apathy that had numbed their hearts gave way to purpose. They experienced firsthand that peace doesn't come from control, but from *surrender*—from making Christ the unseen head of the home.

Turning Homes into Spiritual Greenhouses

When we think of a greenhouse, we think of a nurturing space where plants grow in protection, warmth, and light—shielded from harsh conditions outside. In the same way, a spiritual greenhouse home protects the hearts of children from the cold winds of culture and the storms of confusion.

Parents cannot control the world their children live in, but they can cultivate the world within their walls. Every word spoken, every act of kindness, every prayer whispered adds spiritual oxygen to the home.

Paul described the household of faith beautifully when he wrote, *"Let the peace of Christ rule in your hearts… and be thankful. Let the word of Christ dwell in you richly"* (Colossians 3:15–16). When peace rules, and the Word dwells richly, the house becomes holy ground.

10 Ways to Make Your Home a Spiritual Greenhouse

(A ready-to-use reflective checklist for families)

1. **Dedicate your home to God** — *Pray over every room, inviting the Holy Spirit to dwell there.*
2. **Keep worship central** — *Play worship music in the background; let praise fill the air instead of noise or gossip.*
3. **Prioritize mealtime fellowship** — *At least one meal a day together; no devices, no rush—just conversation and gratitude.*
4. **Pray together daily** — *Short, sincere prayers as a family can do more than long, formal ones done alone.*
5. **Speak words of blessing** — *Replace complaints with declarations of faith. Speak God's promises aloud over your children.*
6. **Read Scripture aloud** — *Let every member, even children, take turns reading and reflecting.*
7. **Deal with conflict quickly** — *Don't let the sun go down on anger (Ephesians 4:26). Seek forgiveness fast.*
8. **Model what you teach** — *Children learn more from what they see than what they hear.*
9. **Create a faith corner** — *A small space with a Bible, cross, or prayer jar—reminding everyone that Christ is the center.*
10. **Celebrate spiritual milestones** — *Baptisms, answered prayers, or even small acts of kindness—mark them together as family testimonies.*

Closing Reflection

A godly home doesn't happen by accident; it's built intentionally, brick by brick, prayer by prayer. A spiritual atmosphere is not the absence of trouble—it is the *presence of God* in the midst of it.

When the storms of life hit, homes rooted in God's Word will stand strong. Like Timothy's home under Lois and Eunice, your home too can raise generations whose faith echoes long after you're gone.

So let your home ring with laughter, worship, and prayer. Let it be said of your household:

"This is a place where the Lord is honored. This is a house that serves the King."

And in Heaven's eyes, that home will forever shine as a beacon of light in a dark world.

The Role of the Church and Community

Key Verse: *Mark 10:14 – "Let the little children come to Me, and do not hinder them, for the kingdom of God belongs to such as these."*

The Forgotten Frontline

If one were to walk into most churches on a Sunday morning, they would likely find the main sanctuary filled with worshippers, the choir passionately singing, and the pastor delivering the Word with conviction. But somewhere down a hallway, behind brightly painted doors, there's another gathering—a smaller one, filled with laughter, crayons, and restless energy. That's the children's ministry.

For years, this ministry has too often been viewed as a *side department*, a babysitting zone to keep children occupied while "the real church" happens elsewhere. Yet, Jesus saw it very differently. When the disciples tried to send the children away, seeing them as a distraction to Jesus' serious ministry, He rebuked them: *"Let the little children come to Me, and do not hinder them, for the kingdom of God belongs to such as these"* (Mark 10:14).

That single statement redefined the value of children in the Kingdom of God. Jesus didn't just tolerate children—He welcomed them. He didn't see them as the church *of tomorrow*; He saw them as an integral part of the church *today.*

The truth is, children's ministry is not the church's side project—it is the frontline of spiritual warfare for the next generation.

When the Church Sees Children as Its Mission Field

Every church has a mission field. For some, it's the urban poor. For others, it's the unreached nations. But the most accessible, fertile, and neglected mission field is often sitting within the church's own walls—its children.

When children are taught the truth early, they grow up anchored in identity and purpose. When neglected, they grow up searching for those things in the wrong places. Proverbs 22:6 reminds us, *"Train up a child in the way he should go, and when he is old, he will not depart from it."* The verse doesn't say "hope" or "pray" he will not depart—it says *train* him. That word "train" implies intentionality, structure, and consistency.

In the Old Testament, we find a powerful example in the life of Samuel. As a young boy, his mother Hannah dedicated him to the Lord's service, and he grew up in the temple under Eli's mentorship. While others slept, Samuel learned to hear God's voice in the night (1 Samuel 3). The temple was more than a place of worship—it was Samuel's classroom for destiny.

Similarly, when the church today becomes a training ground instead of a weekend amusement park, children begin to discover their spiritual calling early.

Case Example: Pastor Grace's Church – From Entertainment to Empowerment

For years, Pastor Grace's church, *FaithLight Community Church*, ran what they called a "Children's Hour." It was a colorful, activity-based time filled with games, cartoons, and snacks. Parents appreciated the distraction—it kept their kids busy while they attended the adult service. But something didn't sit right with Pastor Grace.

One Sunday, as she observed the children's wing, she realized that while the kids were laughing and playing, none of them were learning the Word. There was noise, but no transformation. That week, she gathered her children's ministry team and said, "We're not babysitters. We are builders of faith. These children must encounter God here."

They decided to overhaul the program completely. Instead of entertainment-based sessions, they introduced worship, storytelling, and practical lessons of faith. Each child received a "Mission Journal" where they recorded prayers, memory verses, and acts of kindness they had done each week.

Within months, the change was visible. One nine-year-old boy named Ethan prayed for his sick grandmother and saw her recover. A shy girl, Hannah, began leading worship choruses with confidence. The children were no longer passive attendees—they were becoming disciples.

When parents started noticing their kids quoting scripture at home, praying for their meals voluntarily, and asking deep questions about God, the church realized what had truly happened: the children's ministry had become a mission-focused discipleship model.

Mentorship, Integration, and Intergenerational Worship

The body of Christ was never meant to be divided by age. Psalm 145:4 declares, *"One generation shall commend your works to another and shall declare your mighty acts."* Every generation in the church has a role—elders provide wisdom, adults provide example, and children bring purity and passion.

When churches create spaces where generations worship together, the Kingdom becomes visible in its fullness.

Take for instance King Josiah, who became king of Judah at just eight years old (2 Kings 22:1). Surrounded by older priests and prophets like Hilkiah and Huldah, Josiah led one of the most powerful revivals in Israel's history. Though young, he was not dismissed; he was *guided and mentored.*

That's the essence of intergenerational ministry — the wisdom of elders empowering the zeal of youth.

In one community church, an older couple named Daniel and Mary, both in their seventies, volunteered to mentor pre-teens in prayer and worship. Every Saturday, they met a group of twelve children for what they called *"Kingdom Conversations."* They prayed together, shared testimonies, and learned Bible truths through storytelling. Years later, several of those children became youth leaders, one even a missionary in another country. Daniel and Mary understood a truth many overlook: mentorship builds bridges that sermons alone cannot.

Training Teachers and Volunteers for Spiritual Impact

The strength of a children's ministry lies not in its curriculum but in its people. Teachers and volunteers are the *spiritual gardeners* of young hearts. A seed planted in Sunday School can bear fruit decades later. But that depends on who plants it.

In many churches, volunteers are chosen because they "like kids" or have "free time." But loving children is not enough; teaching them spiritual truth requires calling, preparation, and prayer.

Ephesians 6:4 gives a divine pattern: *"Bring them up in the nurture and admonition of the Lord."* The word "nurture" speaks of care and relationship; "admonition" speaks of truth and instruction. Both are needed.

At *Living Word Fellowship*, Pastor Nathan implemented a simple but powerful model for children's ministry volunteers. Every teacher had to go through a three-step preparation process:

- ✓ **Spiritual Alignment** – Each volunteer spent a week in personal devotion and prayer, asking God for a heart for children.
- ✓ **Scripture Training** – They attended short workshops on teaching the Bible in age-appropriate ways.
- ✓ **Mentorship Commitment** – Every teacher was assigned five children to pray for by name weekly.

Six months later, the testimonies began pouring in. Children were quoting verses in school, leading prayer circles, and even asking for Bibles for their friends. Pastor Nathan realized that trained, prayerful volunteers multiply Kingdom impact far beyond the classroom.

Creating Church Environments that Nurture, Not Entertain

We live in a culture obsessed with entertainment, and sadly, that mindset has crept into the church. Many ministries equate engagement with flashing lights, puppets, or videos. But spiritual growth does not come from stimulation—it comes from *encounter.*

Jesus never entertained the crowds; He engaged them. He told stories, asked questions, and revealed truth in ways that changed hearts.

A nurturing church environment prioritizes presence over performance. It focuses on prayer, Scripture, and relationship. It's a place where children don't just *hear* about God—they *experience* Him.

When the Spirit of God moves in children's ministry, even the smallest hearts sense His touch. I once heard of a little boy, Samuel, only six years old, who, during worship, began to cry softly. His teacher asked if he was alright. He said, "I just feel Jesus here." That's not emotion—that's *encounter*. And that's what the church must pursue.

The Power of Community Support

The phrase *"it takes a village to raise a child"* may not come from the Bible, but its truth echoes Scripture. The church is that spiritual village—a community of faith where every member has a part to play in shaping the next generation.

When a child walks into church, they should feel not like visitors, but like *heirs of the Kingdom*. When parents bring their children, they shouldn't feel relief ("finally, a break!") but partnership ("we're in this together").

Hebrews 10:24–25 reminds us, *"Let us consider how we may spur one another on toward love and good deeds… encouraging one another."* This includes encouraging our children to love, serve, and live for Christ.

Churches that embrace this mindset create ecosystems where faith grows naturally.

Practical Tools for Churches and Ministries

Curriculum Ideas

- ✓ Use story-based learning from Scripture—stories of courage, faith, and obedience.
- ✓ Include "Faith in Action" projects—visiting the sick, writing cards to missionaries, or collecting food for the needy.
- ✓ Encourage Scripture memorization with creative methods like song, drama, and art.

Prayer Models

- ✓ Begin every children's session with an *invocation prayer*: "Holy Spirit, teach us today."
- ✓ Have "Blessing Circles" at the end—teachers pray individually over each child.
- ✓ Create intercessory chains where church members pray weekly for children by name.

Volunteer Training Checklist

- ✓ Are you walking closely with God?
- ✓ Do you pray daily for the children under your care?
- ✓ Do you prepare spiritually before each lesson?
- ✓ Are you modeling Christlike character?
- ✓ Do you listen and love with patience?

These are not rules—they are spiritual disciplines that transform ministry into mission.

The Church as a Training Ground for Kingdom Warriors

The greatest revival the world will ever see may not start on a pulpit but in a children's classroom. When the church begins to view children's ministry as *frontline ministry*, everything changes.

Jesus didn't call for scholars or soldiers—He called for *childlike hearts.* He said, *"Whoever welcomes one such child in My name welcomes Me"* (Matthew 18:5). To welcome a child into the presence of God is to welcome God Himself into the church.

So may every church rise up to its true calling:

To raise worshippers, warriors, and witnesses—starting from the smallest among them.

Because when we win the children, we win the future.

Practical Toolkit:
The Church Resource Pack

1. CHILDREN'S MINISTRY CURRICULUM FRAMEWORK

A framework to turn Sunday school into a discipleship movement.

A. Vision Statement

"To raise children who love Jesus deeply, live by His Word, and lead others by their example."

B. Foundational Scripture:

Mark 10:14 – "Let the little children come to Me, and do not hinder them, for the kingdom of God belongs to such as these."

C. Core Pillars of the Curriculum (The 4D Model)

Discover God's Word

Children learn key Bible stories with a "God connection" — what it teaches about His nature.

Example: Creation (Genesis 1) → *"God made me and everything with love and order."*

Develop Godly Character

- ✓ Focus on virtues like honesty, kindness, and forgiveness.
- ✓ Weekly activities (dramas, drawings, real-life stories) to internalize values.
- ✓ *Example:* Joseph forgives his brothers (Genesis 50:20) → *"I can forgive because God forgave me."*

Deepen Relationship through Worship & Prayer

- ✓ Teach children to talk to God naturally.
- ✓ Use "Prayer Corners" and simple worship songs.
- ✓ Encourage journaling or drawing "God moments."

Deploy to Influence the World

- ✓ Challenge children to *live out* faith at school and home.
- ✓ Teach service, kindness projects, and boldness in truth.
- ✓ *Example:* The little maid who helped Naaman (2 Kings 5) → *"Even small acts can reveal God's power."*

D. Sample 4-Week Lesson Plan: "I Belong to God's Kingdom"

Week	Theme	Key Verse	Bible Story	Activity
1	God Made Me	Psalm 139:14	Creation	"Mirror Craft" – Write "I am God's masterpiece."
2	Jesus Loves Me	John 3:16	Jesus & the Children	Heart cut-outs with names and blessings
3	I Can Hear God	1 Sam 3:10	Samuel's Call	"Quiet Time" listening exercise
4	I Can Shine for God	Matt 5:16	Light of the World	Candlelight circle prayer

Each week ends with a Family Challenge Card to take home — e.g., *"Pray with your parents for one friend this week."*

---

2. PRAYER TEMPLATE PACK FOR VOLUNTEERS & TEACHERS

A. Before the Service (Preparation Prayer)

"Heavenly Father, thank You for the children You entrust to us today.
Help us to see each child as You see them — precious, purposeful, and full of potential.
Fill us with Your Spirit to teach with joy, patience, and truth.
Let every song, story, and smile reveal Jesus. Amen."

B. During the Service (Discernment Prayer)

"Lord, open our eyes to sense when a child is hurting, confused, or hungry for You. Give us words of encouragement and wisdom beyond our own. May this room be a sanctuary of love, not performance — of truth, not distraction."

C. After the Service (Blessing & Release Prayer)

"Father, seal the Word planted in each heart today. May these seeds grow into trees of righteousness. We bless every family represented here and declare that no weapon formed against these children shall prosper (Isaiah 54:17). In Jesus' Name, Amen."

---

3. THE "BLESSING CIRCLE" GUIDE FOR SERVICES

A powerful closing practice that releases the prophetic blessing over every child.

Purpose:

To create a sacred moment each week where children tangibly experience God's love and affirmation through spoken blessing.

How It Works:

Gathering:

After worship or teaching, form a circle (or several small circles).
Teachers and pastors stand with the children.

Declaration of Identity:

Together, everyone says aloud:

"I am a child of God. I am loved, chosen, and created for His purpose!"

Scripture Blessing:

Leader reads aloud:

"May the Lord bless you and keep you; may His face shine upon you and give you peace." (Numbers 6:24–26)

Personal Blessing Moment:
Each child is gently prayed over by name.
Example blessing:
"Daniel, you are called to be a light in your school. God's courage and wisdom rest upon you."
"Grace, the joy of the Lord will be your strength wherever you go."
Anointing Option (Monthly Service):
Use a drop of oil to anoint the forehead with the sign of the cross, declaring:
"You belong to Jesus — may His Spirit lead you always."
Parent Involvement:
Once a month, parents join the circle to speak blessings over their own children — creating intergenerational ministry unity.

---

4. VOLUNTEER TRAINING CHECKLIST

Focus Area	Key Actions	Scripture Anchor
Spiritual Preparation	Daily prayer, fasting once a month	Psalm 78:4
Child Safety	Follow protocols, respect every child	Proverbs 4:23
Teaching	Keep Christ central in every activity	Colossians 1:28
Engagement	Use visuals, questions, and storytelling	Deut. 6:7
Nurture	Encourage, listen, affirm	1 Thess. 5:11

---

5. ADDITIONAL RESOURCES FOR CHURCH LEADERS

Quarterly Parent Connect Nights: Bring parents and ministry volunteers together for prayer and vision alignment.

Mentorship Circles: Pair older youth (ages 13–18) with younger kids for mentorship and prayer partnerships.

Faith Journals: Encourage children to record answered prayers and Bible verses in their own "God Journal."

Annual "Blessing Service": Dedicate one Sunday each year to speak prophetic blessings over all children and teens — commissioning them for their schools and futures.

Final Declaration for the Church

"Father, thank You for trusting us with Your treasures — Your children.
We commit to raise, equip, and release them as arrows in Your hand (Psalm 127:4).
Let our churches become training grounds for Kingdom builders, not playgrounds for mere activity.
May every seed sown in a child's heart bring forth a harvest that shapes nations for Your glory."

The Power of Blessing and Declaration

Key Verse*: "Death and life are in the power of the tongue: and they that love it shall eat the fruit thereof." — Proverbs 18:21 (KJV)*

From the very beginning, God demonstrated the creative power of words. He spoke, and light appeared. He declared, and creation took form. Every mountain, ocean, and living being came into existence because of a spoken word. This is the same power—though on a smaller scale—that God has entrusted to parents, teachers, and leaders when shaping the lives of children. Words are never neutral; they either build or break, bless or curse, release faith or fear.

In every home, there is a constant spiritual transaction taking place through speech. The tone, words, and declarations spoken daily over a child form unseen walls of faith, courage, or insecurity. Many parents unknowingly prophesy fear or limitation over their children through careless speech—phrases like *"You're so lazy," "You'll never change,"* or *"You're just like your father/mother"* carry immense spiritual weight. Yet the opposite is equally true: words of blessing can ignite destiny, unlock confidence, and remind a child who they are in God's eyes.

1. Words Shape Destiny: Parents and Leaders as Prophets

In Scripture, parents and patriarchs often acted as prophets over their households. Jacob, in Genesis 49, gathered his twelve sons to declare what would "befall them in the days to come." Those were not casual words—they were destinies spoken into being. Each declaration contained a prophetic insight, a shaping of legacy. When he spoke over Judah, saying, *"The scepter shall not depart from Judah,"* it foreshadowed the lineage through which Christ Himself would come.

Similarly, Isaac's blessing over Jacob—though mistakenly given—carried irreversible power (Genesis 27:33). Isaac trembled when he realized he had blessed Jacob instead of Esau, saying, *"Indeed he shall be blessed."* Once spoken, the spiritual authority of the word could not be revoked. This shows us the potency of words released under authority.

In the New Testament, we see Jesus Himself modeling the same principle. When He encountered Simon, He said, *"You are Simon, son of Jonah. You shall be called Peter."* (John 1:42). In that moment, Jesus wasn't describing Simon's current character—impulsive, unstable—but declaring who he would become: *"a rock."*

Every parent has this prophetic privilege. When you look into your child's eyes and speak words of truth—*"You are loved, chosen, wise, and strong in the Lord"*—you are participating in heaven's design for their destiny.

2. The Difference Between Prayer and Prophetic Decree

Prayer seeks heaven's will; declaration releases heaven's authority.

Prayer is asking; declaration is enforcing.

A parent might pray, *"Lord, help my child be strong and bold,"* but when they declare, *"My child is strong and courageous, filled with wisdom and peace,"* they are speaking as ambassadors of the King, enforcing divine truth on earth as it is in heaven (Matthew 6:10).

Both are essential. Prayer aligns the heart; declaration releases the word. Together, they become a two-edged sword (Hebrews 4:12), cutting through spiritual opposition that seeks to derail a child's purpose.

When we speak God's Word over children, we're not merely using positive affirmations—we are invoking divine law. Isaiah 55:11 reminds us, *"So shall My word be that goes forth from My mouth; it shall not return to Me void, but it shall accomplish what I please."*

3. Breaking Word Curses and Negative Labeling

There are homes where children grow under the weight of constant criticism, comparison, or negativity. These words can become invisible chains. Many adults still carry the echoes of phrases spoken over them in childhood—*"You'll never succeed," "You're always a problem," "Why can't you be like your brother?"* These are not just emotional wounds; they are spiritual declarations that need to be renounced.

In the Old Testament, we find that even great men like Jabez suffered from a name that carried a curse. His mother named him Jabez, saying, *"Because I bore him in pain."* Yet Jabez cried out to God, *"Oh, that You would bless me indeed..."* and the Lord granted his request (1 Chronicles 4:9–10). Jabez broke the limiting power of that name through prayer and faith, and his story teaches us that blessings can overturn curses when spoken with faith.

Parents and mentors today can do the same. They can cancel negative words spoken in haste by replacing them with truth-filled declarations. Instead of saying, *"You're impossible,"* one can declare, *"You are growing in patience and understanding."* Instead of, *"You never listen,"* say, *"You have ears that hear the voice of wisdom."*

4. Biblical Example: Jacob Blessing His Sons (Genesis 49)

Jacob's blessing was more than a farewell—it was a spiritual commissioning. Each word was specific, purposeful, and prophetic.

To Reuben, he spoke of instability because of uncontrolled passion—reminding us that our words must also be truthful, guiding correction in love.

To Joseph, he declared abundance and favor: *"The blessings of your father have excelled the blessings of my ancestors."*

Jacob's blessings became living words that followed his sons and their descendants.

Parents today can learn from this. Blessings must be intentional, not vague. They must call out divine qualities, speak to purpose, and set direction. Saying *"God bless you"* is good—but declaring *"You will be a blessing to nations, a carrier of peace, and a light wherever you go"* is prophetic.

5. Real-Life Example: The Daniels Family

Mrs. Daniels was a single mother of two lively boys—Matthew and Joel. Her home was not free from challenges; finances were tight, and she often battled discouragement. Yet every morning before school, she made a habit of speaking blessings over her

sons. She would place her hands on their heads and say,
"You are sons of purpose. You walk in wisdom. You will make choices that please the Lord. You are favored, protected, and filled with peace."
At first, the boys giggled, not understanding why she did this daily. But as the years passed, those words became part of their identity.
Matthew, once timid and unsure, began leading prayer groups in college. Joel, who struggled with anger, grew into a gentle encourager among his peers. When asked what made the difference, both boys pointed back to their mother's words. *"Mom didn't just pray for us,"* Joel said, *"She spoke who we were before we even saw it."*
Blessings build an inner compass. They give children a picture of who they are in God's sight long before the world tries to redefine them.

6. Practical Toolkit: Daily Declarations for Parents to Speak

Below are sample declarations you can personalize for your children. These are not magic words—they are faith-filled confessions grounded in Scripture. Speak them with conviction, often aloud, believing that heaven responds.
Morning Blessings (Before School):

- ✓ *"You are the head and not the tail (Deut. 28:13). You walk in wisdom, strength, and favor today."*
- ✓ *"You are surrounded by angels; no harm shall befall you (Psalm 91:11)."*
- ✓ *"Your mind is alert, your heart is pure, and your hands are diligent."*

Evening Blessings (Before Bed):

- ✓ *"You sleep in peace and safety because the Lord is your shepherd (Psalm 4:8)."*
- ✓ *"Your dreams are filled with light, and your future is secure in God's hands."*
- ✓ *"You are loved deeply, chosen eternally, and destined for greatness."*

Identity Declarations (Spoken Regularly):

- ✓ *"You are God's masterpiece (Ephesians 2:10)."*
- ✓ *"You are bold as a lion and gentle as a dove."*
- ✓ *"The Holy Spirit guides you, teaches you, and strengthens you daily."*

7. Speaking Life Over the Next Generation

Imagine if every home, every Sunday school, every classroom began to echo with declarations of life instead of frustration. Imagine a generation rising up who have heard, since childhood, *"You are chosen. You are called. You are loved."*

That is what God desires. Proverbs 22:6 says, *"Train up a child in the way he should go, and when he is old, he will not depart from it."* Training includes teaching, example, and declaration.

We are not merely raising children—we are raising prophets, leaders, and ambassadors of God's Kingdom. And one of the most powerful tools we have been given is the spoken word. Every blessing you release today becomes a seed in their tomorrow. So, speak life. Speak destiny. Speak blessing—until your home resounds with the language of heaven.

31 Days of Daily Declarations

Building Powerful Children – One Blessing at a Time
(For Parents, Teachers & Guardians)

DAY 1
Morning: *"You are fearfully and wonderfully made by God." (Psalm 139:14)*
Bedtime: *"God watches over you while you sleep." (Psalm 121:3–4)*
Identity: *"You are God's masterpiece, created for His good works." (Ephesians 2:10)*

DAY 2
Morning: *"The Lord is your Shepherd; you will not lack anything today." (Psalm 23:1)*
Bedtime: *"God surrounds you with His angels tonight." (Psalm 91:11)*
Identity: *"You belong to Jesus; you are safe in His arms." (John 10:28)*

DAY 3
Morning: *"God's mercy is new for you this morning." (Lamentations 3:22–23)*
Bedtime: *"You will lie down and sleep in peace." (Psalm 4:8)*
Identity: *"You are chosen and dearly loved." (Colossians 3:12)*

DAY 4
Morning: *"You are strong and courageous, for God is with you." (Joshua 1:9)*
Bedtime: *"The Lord gives His beloved sweet rest." (Psalm 127:2)*

Identity: *"You are more than a conqueror through Christ." (Romans 8:37)*

DAY 5

Morning: *"God's joy is your strength today." (Nehemiah 8:10)*
Bedtime: *"God quiets you with His love tonight." (Zephaniah 3:17)*
Identity: *"You are filled with the joy of the Lord." (John 15:11)*

DAY 6

Morning: *"The Lord blesses the work of your hands." (Deut. 28:12)*
Bedtime: *"May your dreams be filled with God's goodness." (Psalm 16:7)*
Identity: *"You are a blessing and not a burden." (Genesis 12:2)*

DAY 7

Morning: *"You are surrounded by God's favor as a shield." (Psalm 5:12)*
Bedtime: *"The Lord is your refuge and fortress." (Psalm 91:2)*
Identity: *"You are protected by God's power." (1 Peter 1:5)*

DAY 8

Morning: *"You will walk in wisdom and kindness today." (Proverbs 3:3–4)*
Bedtime: *"The Lord keeps you in perfect peace." (Isaiah 26:3)*
Identity: *"You are filled with the wisdom of God." (James 1:5)*

DAY 9

Morning: *"Your steps are ordered by the Lord." (Psalm 37:23)*

Bedtime: *"God holds you close and never lets you go." (Deut. 33:27)*

Identity: *"You are guided by the Holy Spirit." (Romans 8:14)*

DAY 10

Morning: *"The Lord delights in you today." (Zephaniah 3:17)*

Bedtime: *"You rest in His love and care." (Psalm 4:8)*

Identity: *"You are deeply loved by your Heavenly Father." (1 John 3:1)*

DAY 11

Morning: *"You are a light in the world today." (Matthew 5:14)*

Bedtime: *"Even in the dark, God's light shines on you." (Psalm 139:12)*

Identity: *"You are a carrier of God's light." (Philippians 2:15)*

DAY 12

Morning: *"The Lord gives you peace that passes understanding." (Philippians 4:7)*

Bedtime: *"His peace guards your heart tonight." (John 14:27)*

Identity: *"You are a peacemaker, a child of God." (Matthew 5:9)*

DAY 13
Morning: *"You can do all things through Christ who strengthens you." (Philippians 4:13)*
Bedtime: *"The Lord renews your strength while you rest." (Isaiah 40:31)*
Identity: *"You are strong in the Lord." (Ephesians 6:10)*

DAY 14
Morning: *"God's grace covers you today." (2 Corinthians 12:9)*
Bedtime: *"His goodness and mercy follow you always." (Psalm 23:6)*
Identity: *"You are covered by grace and clothed in righteousness." (Isaiah 61:10)*

DAY 15
Morning: *"You are fruitful in every good work." (Colossians 1:10)*
Bedtime: *"Your rest brings refreshment for tomorrow's fruit." (Psalm 92:12–14)*
Identity: *"You are planted in the house of the Lord." (Psalm 92:13)*

DAY 16
Morning: *"God gives you a sound mind and a joyful heart." (2 Timothy 1:7)*
Bedtime: *"The Lord's peace rests upon your thoughts." (Isaiah 26:3)*
Identity: *"You are filled with love, power, and sound mind." (2 Timothy 1:7)*

DAY 17
Morning: *"You are called to be a leader and example." (1 Timothy 4:12)*

Bedtime: *"God is pleased with your obedience." (John 14:23)*
Identity: *"You are chosen to lead others to Jesus." (Matthew 28:19)*

DAY 18
Morning: *"You will walk in truth and integrity today." (Proverbs 10:9)*
Bedtime: *"God rejoices in your honesty." (Psalm 51:6)*
Identity: *"You are a child of truth." (John 8:32)*

DAY 19
Morning: *"You will love others as God loves you." (John 15:12)*
Bedtime: *"The Lord fills your heart with compassion." (Colossians 3:12)*
Identity: *"You are kind, gentle, and full of love." (Galatians 5:22–23)*

DAY 20
Morning: *"The Lord establishes the work of your hands." (Psalm 90:17)*
Bedtime: *"God blesses your learning and rest." (Proverbs 3:24)*
Identity: *"You are blessed to be a blessing." (Genesis 12:2)*

DAY 21
Morning: *"God's presence goes with you today." (Exodus 33:14)*
Bedtime: *"You sleep in the shelter of His wings." (Psalm 91:4)*
Identity: *"You are never alone — God is with you." (Matthew 28:20)*

DAY 22
Morning: *"You have the mind of Christ." (1 Corinthians 2:16)*
Bedtime: *"God fills your dreams with His wisdom." (Proverbs 3:24)*
Identity: *"You are smart, creative, and full of divine ideas." (Daniel 1:17)*

DAY 23
Morning: *"You are an overcomer in every challenge." (1 John 5:4)*
Bedtime: *"God gives you courage to face tomorrow." (Psalm 56:3–4)*
Identity: *"You are victorious in Christ Jesus." (Romans 8:37)*

DAY 24
Morning: *"The Lord teaches and guides you in all things." (Psalm 32:8)*
Bedtime: *"You rest knowing God leads your path." (Proverbs 3:6)*
Identity: *"You are guided by His wisdom every day." (James 1:5)*

DAY 25
Morning: *"You shine bright for Jesus wherever you go." (Matthew 5:16)*
Bedtime: *"Your light never goes out in God's eyes." (Proverbs 31:18)*
Identity: *"You are the light of the world." (John 8:12)*

DAY 26
Morning: *"God gives you favor with friends, teachers, and leaders." (Proverbs 3:4)*
Bedtime: *"You are surrounded by His goodness." (Psalm 23:6)*
Identity: *"You are favored and fruitful in God's sight." (Luke 2:52)*

DAY 27
Morning: *"You are filled with courage to do what's right." (Joshua 1:9)*
Bedtime: *"Your heart is strong and fearless in God." (Psalm 27:1)*
Identity: *"You are brave and bold for Jesus." (Acts 4:13)*

DAY 28
Morning: *"God fills you with joy that overflows." (Romans 15:13)*
Bedtime: *"The joy of the Lord refreshes your heart." (Psalm 16:11)*
Identity: *"You are full of joy and gratitude." (1 Thess. 5:16–18)*

DAY 29
Morning: *"You will listen to God's voice today." (John 10:27)*
Bedtime: *"God speaks peace to your heart." (Psalm 85:8)*
Identity: *"You are a listener and follower of the Good Shepherd." (John 10:14)*

DAY 30
Morning: *"You will be a blessing to others today." (Proverbs 11:25)*

Bedtime: *"God multiplies the seeds of kindness you've sown." (Galatians 6:9)*
Identity: *"You are a world changer for God." (Matthew 28:19)*

DAY 31
Morning: *"The Lord has great plans for your life." (Jeremiah 29:11)*
Bedtime: *"God is faithful to complete what He started in you." (Philippians 1:6)*
Identity: *"You are destined for greatness in God's Kingdom." (Romans 8:30)*

How to Use These Cards:

- ✓ **Print and Cut:** Place each card on cardstock and cut into 31 pieces.
- ✓ **Morning Time:** Speak the *Morning Declaration* over your child before school.
- ✓ **Bedtime:** Pray the *Bedtime Blessing* gently before they sleep.
- ✓ **Identity:** Repeat the *Identity Declaration* aloud daily for 31 days — these truths will root deeply in your child's spirit.
- ✓ **After 31 Days:** Shuffle and continue using — these words never expire!

Healing the Wounds of the Past (for Parents and Children)

Key Verse*: "He heals the brokenhearted and binds up their wounds." — Psalm 147:3 (NIV)*

Every home carries a story—some chapters bright and filled with laughter, others shadowed by pain, misunderstandings, or regret. Behind every well-dressed family at church, there are often invisible scars—words once spoken in anger, promises broken, affection withheld, or shame carried silently. Parents carry their own burdens from childhood, and children absorb the residue of those unhealed hurts. These wounds, if left unattended, can quietly distort how both parent and child see themselves and God.

Yet the hope of the Gospel is this: God heals broken hearts. Not only can He redeem a person's individual pain, but He can also restore the very fabric of a family. He specializes in turning mourning into dancing, ashes into beauty, and dysfunction into a testimony of grace. (Isaiah 61:3)

1. Recognizing Hidden Wounds in Families

Emotional wounds are not always visible, but their fruit is unmistakable. A child who was constantly criticized may grow up performing for approval. A father who felt abandoned by his own parents may become distant, repeating the same pattern he once resented. A mother who was never affirmed might overcompensate, becoming controlling or fearful of failure.

These patterns are often generational—cycles of rejection, anger, or fear passed down unconsciously. The Bible calls this "the iniquity of the fathers"

(Exodus 34:7)—not as punishment, but as the natural flow of influence. However, through Christ, those cycles can be broken.

In the Old Testament, Joseph is a powerful example of someone who broke free from the wounds of his past. Betrayed by his brothers, sold into slavery, and wrongfully imprisoned, he had every reason to live in bitterness. Yet when he finally faced his brothers, his words reflected complete healing:

"You meant evil against me, but God meant it for good." (Genesis 50:20)

Joseph's forgiveness turned his pain into purpose. In doing so, he preserved not just his own future, but an entire nation. That's the power of healed hearts—it multiplies blessing instead of pain.

2. The Journey of Forgiveness and Repentance

Forgiveness is not pretending that the hurt never happened. It is acknowledging the pain but choosing to release the offender into God's hands. It is refusing to let bitterness poison the next generation.

In the New Testament, Peter once asked Jesus, *"Lord, how often shall my brother sin against me, and I forgive him? Up to seven times?"* Jesus answered, *"Not seven times, but seventy times seven."* (Matthew 18:21–22).

In other words, forgiveness is not a single act—it's a lifestyle.

Repentance, too, is a healing balm. When a parent humbly admits wrongdoing to a child—"I was harsh, and I am sorry"—something sacred happens. The atmosphere shifts. Walls fall. The child learns that grace is real.

Real-Life Example: Kevin and His Father

Kevin was a quiet twelve-year-old, often withdrawn. His father, Mr. Roy, was a disciplined man who believed in tough love. Every mistake was met with criticism. Kevin began to retreat inward, avoiding conversation and hiding his report cards out of fear.

One Sunday, their pastor preached on *"The Father Heart of God."* Convicted deeply, Mr. Roy went home and knelt before his son. With tears in his eyes, he said, "Kevin, I have been harsh and unkind. I thought I was teaching you responsibility, but I've wounded you. Will you forgive me?"

Kevin didn't answer immediately. But as his father embraced him, years of tension broke. Both wept—father and son held together by grace. In the months that followed, Kevin's confidence bloomed. His father began blessing him daily, and their home became filled with warmth that had long been missing.

Healing began not with perfection, but with humility.

3. God's Healing Through Truth, Worship, and Love

The Holy Spirit often begins His work of restoration in the most unexpected ways—a song, a sermon, a conversation, or even a moment of silence in prayer. Worship has a unique power to bring healing because it shifts our gaze from pain to the presence of God.

David, who knew deep wounds of betrayal and loss, wrote, *"The Lord is near to the brokenhearted and saves those who are crushed in spirit."* (Psalm 34:18). In his psalms, David processed pain through worship. He cried, questioned, and confessed—but always returned to hope. This teaches us that healing doesn't require perfection; it requires honesty before God.

Truth is another instrument of healing. Jesus said, *"You shall know the truth, and the truth shall make you free."* (John 8:32). Many families live under lies—*"I'll never change," "Our family has always been this way," "Some wounds can't heal."* These are not truths; they are chains. The truth is that Christ redeems every broken piece.

Love completes the process. 1 Peter 4:8 says, *"Love covers a multitude of sins."* Love does not erase accountability, but it gives room for grace to work. When parents model love, children learn to forgive faster, trust deeper, and grow stronger.

4. Rebuilding Faith and Confidence

When the past is healed, faith is rekindled. Many children struggle to believe in a loving God because they've been hurt by unloving authority figures. When a father or mother repents and restores relationship, it becomes a living picture of God's heart.

We see this in Jesus' parable of the Prodigal Son (Luke 15:11–24). The father did not wait for his son to crawl back in shame; he ran to meet him, restored him with a robe, and reinstated him as a son. That's what God does—and it's what parents are called to reflect. Restoration restores not only relationship but also identity and destiny.

One mother, Mrs. Anita, experienced this when her teenage daughter, Mia, rebelled against the family's faith. After months of conflict, Anita stopped trying to lecture her and instead began to pray and bless her quietly. One night, she whispered to God, "I release her into Your love." Weeks later, Mia unexpectedly joined her for church. The sermon that day was on forgiveness—and both mother and daughter ended up at the altar, weeping together. Their relationship was never the same again. Healing flowed when love replaced control.

5. A Practical Guide: Steps for Family Emotional Healing and Reconciliation

Healing in families is not automatic; it must be pursued intentionally, under the guidance of the Holy Spirit. The following process can serve as a simple roadmap for those ready to begin.

Step 1: Honest Acknowledgment

Bring the pain into the light. Denial keeps wounds infected. Families can gather and openly share what has hurt them, without blame. This act itself breaks the power of secrecy.

Step 2: Confession and Repentance

Parents should model humility first. A simple "I was wrong" can unlock decades of silence. Repentance invites grace into the home.

Step 3: Forgiveness

Forgiveness is not forgetting; it's releasing. Say aloud, *"I forgive you, and I bless you."* This breaks emotional chains and invites peace.

Step 4: Blessing and Restoration

Seal the process with words of blessing. Parents can lay hands on their children and declare life-giving truths:

"You are loved. You are secure. You are not defined by past pain. God's plan for you is good."

Step 5: Worship and Communion Together

End the process in worship. Families can sing together or take communion, acknowledging that the blood of Jesus unites and heals.

6. Biblical and Spiritual Reflection

In both Old and New Testaments, God's heart has always been to restore what is broken. When Israel strayed, He sent prophets not only with warnings but with promises of renewal: *"I will restore to you the years that the locust has eaten."* (Joel 2:25).

Jesus, when He read Isaiah's prophecy in the synagogue, declared His mission: *"He has sent Me to heal the brokenhearted."* (Luke 4:18). Every miracle He performed—every blind eye opened, every leper cleansed, every sinner forgiven—was an act of emotional and spiritual restoration.

This same Jesus now desires to walk through the hallways of our homes, touching old wounds and breathing new life. Healing the past is not about reliving pain; it's about reclaiming joy and purpose.

7. A Final Word of Hope

Every family has a past, but in Christ, no past is too broken for restoration. Healing begins the moment we invite Jesus into the painful places we've tried to hide. His love is patient, His forgiveness endless, and His power limitless.

When parents heal, children flourish. When children forgive, homes are reborn. The walls of silence fall, and what remains is a testimony of grace that can ripple through generations.

So today, begin where you are. Speak the words that need to be said. Offer forgiveness. Receive it. And let the Great Physician—Jesus Himself—do what only He can do: bind up the brokenhearted and make all things new.

A Call to the Builders — Parents, Mentors, Teachers, Leaders

Key Verse: *"For every house is built by someone, but God is the builder of everything." — Hebrews 3:4 (NIV)*

Every generation faces a divine summons—a call to build what has been broken and to raise what has fallen. Today, that summons is directed toward parents, mentors, teachers, and leaders: *"Build My children. Build My future."*

In a world where the foundation of family and faith is being shaken, God is looking for modern-day builders—men and women who, like Nehemiah, will rise from comfort to construction, from apathy to action. These builders are not architects of stone, but shapers of souls; not masons of walls, but molders of hearts. They see beyond the chaos of the present to the Kingdom potential within every child.

Children are not merely "the next generation" — they are *this* generation's greatest assignment. Every believer, whether a parent or not, has a role in shaping their future. The call to build is not optional; it's sacred.

1. The Builder's Mandate

When God calls His people "builders," He's not talking about physical structures but *spiritual legacies*. From Genesis to Revelation, the story of Scripture is a story of building — families, covenants, nations, and faith itself.

In Hebrews 3:4, we are reminded that while humans may build houses, *"God is the builder of everything."* That means we are not called to construct in our own strength but to partner with the Master Builder Himself. Parents, mentors, teachers, and leaders are *co-laborers* with God in shaping the next generation's destiny.

Think about Noah, who built an ark that not only saved his family but preserved a righteous seed for generations (Genesis 6:14–22). Noah's obedience was not just about survival—it was about legacy.

Or consider Abraham, who "commanded his children and his household after him to keep the way of the Lord" (Genesis 18:19). His faith built a lineage that became a nation.

And then there is Nehemiah, whose story mirrors the call to every believer today. When he saw the walls of Jerusalem broken down, his heart broke too. But instead of complaining, he prayed, planned, and began to rebuild. He faced opposition, ridicule, and fatigue, yet he persisted until the walls stood strong again. Nehemiah understood something vital: what is left broken in one generation will burden the next—unless someone decides to rebuild.

That's our calling as well: to rebuild the moral, spiritual, and emotional walls around our children before the enemy breaks in.

2. Building Hearts: The Inner Construction

Every child's heart is a construction site. From the moment they are born, walls of trust, love, and faith begin to form. Parents are the first architects. Their words are like bricks; their example is the cement that holds it all together.

In Proverbs 24:3–4, we read:

"By wisdom a house is built, and through understanding it is established; through knowledge its rooms are filled with rare and beautiful treasures."

Building hearts begins with wisdom—teaching children God's truth through everyday living. It's not about grand sermons but small, consistent deposits: bedtime prayers, gentle corrections, listening to their fears, affirming their worth.

Biblical Example:

Think of Hannah, who prayed fervently for a child and then dedicated Samuel to God (1 Samuel 1:27–28). She didn't just give birth to a boy; she birthed a prophet. Her prayers and surrender built in him a heart that would one day hear the voice of God as a child (1 Samuel 3).

Real-Life Example:

Maria and Peter were a young couple who worked long hours. Their son, Ethan, often felt unseen. One night, Maria read Proverbs 22:6 — *"Train up a child in the way he should go..."* — and it pierced her heart. She began setting aside 15 minutes each night to pray with Ethan before bed, asking him about his day and thanking God for one thing. Slowly, those moments softened Ethan's guarded heart. Within months, his teachers noticed a change—he was more confident, kinder, and peaceful. Maria hadn't built a mansion; she built a heart.

Building hearts is slow, holy work—but it's what forms world changers.

3. Building Faith: Foundations That Last

Faith is the strongest wall any builder can erect. Every child must be taught *not just what to believe, but why they believe.* Faith must be experienced, not memorized.

In the New Testament, Paul reminds young Timothy of his spiritual heritage:

"The faith that first dwelt in your grandmother Lois and in your mother Eunice, and I am persuaded, now lives in you also." — 2 Timothy 1:5

Lois and Eunice were builders. They didn't preach from pulpits, but their daily devotion, prayers, and example built a faith that outlived them. They taught Timothy to trust God long before Paul ever mentored him.

Faith builders show children how to respond when life shakes them. They teach them that prayer is not a ritual but a relationship, that God's promises are not abstract, but personal.

Real-Life Example:

John and Angela, Sunday school teachers, decided to start a "Faith Builders Club" in their local church. Every week, children shared one story of how they saw God work during the week—a prayer answered, a friend helped, a fear overcome. One Sunday, eight-year-old Tara shared how she prayed for her sick grandmother and she recovered. The joy on her face lit up the room. That's what faith building looks like—one testimony, one answered prayer at a time.

4. Building the Future: Equipping for Purpose

Builders don't just construct for today—they plan for tomorrow. Likewise, spiritual builders must look beyond present obedience to future destiny. Every child is born with divine purpose. Our role is to help uncover it.

Jeremiah 1:5 declares:

"Before I formed you in the womb, I knew you; before you were born, I set you apart."

Purpose is not discovered accidentally—it's revealed intentionally. Parents, teachers, and mentors must speak life over children's gifts, encourage their creativity, and nurture leadership from a young age.

Biblical Example:

When Jesus called His disciples, He didn't see fishermen—He saw apostles. He said, *"Follow Me, and I will make you fishers of men."* (Matthew 4:19). In that one statement, He redefined their purpose. That's what godly builders do—they see what could be, not just what is.

Real-Life Example:

Mr. David, a high school teacher, noticed that one of his students, Jonah, was unusually compassionate toward others. While Jonah struggled academically, he had a heart that noticed when others were in pain. Instead of focusing on his weaknesses, Mr. David encouraged Jonah to lead a small group for new students. Over time, Jonah's confidence grew, and years later, he became a youth counselor. One teacher's prophetic insight built a destiny.

5. Partnering with God: The Builder's Blueprint

To build effectively, we must follow the Master Builder's plan. Even Nehemiah prayed before laying a single stone. Builders who rely on human wisdom construct temporary walls; those who build with God create eternal legacies.

In Psalm 127:1, we are reminded:

"Unless the Lord builds the house, the builders labor in vain."

True building begins in prayer. Parents should ask:

- ✓ *"Lord, what are You building in my child?"*
- ✓ *"What strengths have You placed in them?"*
- ✓ *"How can I cooperate with Your design?"*

When we build *with* God, He supplies the wisdom, patience, and grace required for the task. He even redeems the broken bricks—our mistakes, regrets, and failures—turning them into testimonies of restoration.

Biblical Parallel:

Just as Noah's obedience secured his family, so does our partnership with God secure the spiritual safety of the next generation. Noah didn't wait for rain to start building; he acted in faith on what God had spoken (Hebrews 11:7). In the same way, we must prepare children for what's coming—even when the world cannot yet see the storm.

6. The Call to Rise and Rebuild

The cry of this generation is not for more entertainment, but for builders—those who will stand in the gap and say, "As for me and my house, we will serve the Lord." (Joshua 24:15)

Children today face crumbling walls—moral confusion, identity struggles, spiritual emptiness. But God is raising Nehemiahs again—parents, teachers, and leaders who will pick up the trowel of truth and rebuild hope, one child at a time.

You may feel unqualified, weary, or too late—but remember: God does not call the equipped; He equips the called. Every prayer whispered over a sleeping child, every Bible story read, every word of encouragement spoken—these are building blocks in the hands of eternity.

Challenge:

What wall will you rebuild in a child's life today?

Is it the wall of faith in your home? The wall of hope in a discouraged heart? The wall of truth in a confused generation? Whatever it is, begin. For the Master Builder stands beside you, tools in hand, whispering, *"Let us rise up and build."* (Nehemiah 2:18)

7. A Final Exhortation

Building children for the Kingdom is not a short project—it's a lifelong calling. You may never see the full structure completed, but your obedience will outlive you. Like Abraham, you are laying foundations for nations you may never see (Hebrews 11:10).

Let your legacy be this: *You built lives, not monuments. You built faith, not fame. You built people who built others.*

And when the Master Builder inspects your work, may He say as He did of Nehemiah's wall, "The work had been done with the help of our God." (Nehemiah 6:16)

The Builder's Mandate Toolkit

1. Parent & Mentor Builder's Prayer

(A prayer of commissioning and surrender for those called to build the next generation)

Heavenly Father,
You are the Master Builder — the One who laid the foundations of the earth and shaped every life with purpose. Today, I stand before You, ready to be Your vessel in building the lives You've entrusted to me.
Lord, give me the wisdom of Nehemiah, the patience of Noah, the faith of Abraham, and the love of Jesus. Help me see every child not as a project, but as a masterpiece in progress — designed by You for greatness.
Teach me to build with truth as my plumb line, **grace** *as my mortar, and faith as my cornerstone. Where I have torn down with harsh words, help me rebuild with healing love. Where walls have been broken, make me a restorer of hope and a repairer of generations.*
Use my home, my classroom, my ministry — as a construction site for eternity.
I declare: I am a builder in the Kingdom of God, and by His grace, I will build lives that last.
In Jesus' Name,
Amen.

---

2. Wall Rebuilding Reflection Sheet

(A reflective journaling tool for parents, teachers, and mentors to identify what "walls" need rebuilding in

their families, classrooms, or ministries — inspired by Nehemiah 2:17–18)

Theme Scripture:

"Come, let us rebuild the wall of Jerusalem, that we may no longer be in disgrace." — Nehemiah 2:17

A. Areas of Broken Walls (Personal Reflection)

Take a moment to prayerfully reflect and write under each point:

- ✓ Walls of Faith: *Have I allowed busyness or doubt to erode family devotion or prayer time?*
- ✓ Walls of Love: *Are there strained relationships that need forgiveness or reconciliation?*
- ✓ Walls of Discipline: *Have I neglected consistency or godly boundaries in raising children?*
- ✓ Walls of Purpose: *Have I helped the next generation see their unique calling in Christ?*
- ✓ Walls of Service: *Am I modeling what it means to serve God joyfully?*

B. God's Call to Action

"The God of heaven Himself will prosper us; therefore we His servants will arise and build." — Nehemiah 2:20

Lord, show me one "wall" I need to start rebuilding this week:

→

____

What first step will I take?

→

____

Who can partner or pray with me as I build?

→

____

C. Declaration:
"By God's grace, I will not just patch what's broken — I will rebuild with purpose, prayer, and perseverance."

---

3. Personal Commitment Declaration – *"I Will Rise and Build"*

(A powerful decree for personal devotion or group commissioning service)

I, (insert name), stand today as a *builder* in the Kingdom of God.
I am called not to tear down, but to raise up; not to neglect, but to nurture; not to consume, but to construct.
I will build:

- ✓ ***Faith*** *in the hearts of my children and those I influence.*
- ✓ ***Character*** *grounded in the Word of God.*
- ✓ ***Relationships*** *founded on grace, truth, and forgiveness.*
- ✓ ***Purpose*** *rooted in the divine blueprint God has for every life.*

I refuse to be silent when the walls crumble. I refuse to stand by while the enemy steals this generation.
I will pray, teach, serve, and lead — until every young life under my care becomes a testimony of God's power.
With the tools of Scripture, prayer, and love in my hands, and the Spirit of the Master Builder within me, I will rise and build — until His Kingdom stands firm through the generations.
"Unless the Lord builds the house, they labor in vain who build it." — Psalm 127:1

Conclusion:
The Future Belongs to the Faithful

Key Verse: *"All your children shall be taught by the Lord, and great shall be the peace of your children."*
— Isaiah 54:13 (NKJV)

The story of God has always been a story of faithfulness — not perfection, not power, not prestige — but steadfast, enduring faithfulness. From one generation to another, the Lord has looked for men and women who would carry His heart, walk in His ways, and pass His truth forward. Every generation rises or falls on the faithfulness of those who came before it. That's why the future — the moral, spiritual, and eternal future — belongs to the faithful.

We live in a time where distractions are louder than devotion, where convenience often trumps conviction, and where many chase success but neglect the soul. Yet amid this noise, God still seeks builders of faith—parents, mentors, teachers, and leaders who will plant righteous seeds in the soil of young hearts. The Kingdom principle remains unchanged:

"The seed you plant today determines tomorrow's harvest."

No one reaps what they did not sow. If we want to see a generation that fears the Lord, walks in truth, and loves righteousness, we must plant those seeds today — not with lectures, but with lives that model Christ.

The Kingdom Law of the Seed

Every great move of God begins small — like a seed. The seed of the Word, the seed of faith, the seed of love. Jesus Himself compared the Kingdom to a mustard seed: tiny in size but mighty in impact (Matthew 13:31–32). The principle is simple: *What you plant today will either feed or starve the future.*

Consider Abraham, called the father of faith. When he obeyed God and left everything familiar to follow an unseen promise (Genesis 12:1–4), he wasn't just making a personal decision. He was planting a generational seed of faith that would one day produce nations. The ripple of his obedience reached Isaac, Jacob, Joseph, Moses, David, and ultimately, Christ Himself. One man's faith became a family legacy.

Likewise, Hannah's prayer for a son wasn't just about her desire for motherhood. When she dedicated Samuel to the Lord (1 Samuel 1:27–28), she sowed a prophetic seed that produced one of Israel's greatest prophets. Hannah's faith shaped history because her seed was holy.

In the New Testament, we see this same pattern. Mary, a humble young woman from Nazareth, said, *"Let it be to me according to your word."* (Luke 1:38). Her obedience brought forth the Savior of the world. Even Jesus Himself described His mission in agricultural terms:

"Unless a grain of wheat falls into the ground and dies, it remains alone; but if it dies, it produces much grain." — John 12:24

The faithful plant in tears, but they always reap in joy (Psalm 126:5).

A Prophetic Declaration for the Next Generation

God's heart for the next generation is beautifully captured in Isaiah 54:13:

“All your children shall be taught by the Lord, and great shall be the peace of your children.”

This is not merely a promise — it’s a prophetic declaration. It declares that children who are taught in the ways of the Lord will not be restless, anxious, or lost. They will be grounded, purposeful, and at peace. But that peace must be cultivated. It doesn’t come by chance; it comes by choice — the choice of parents and leaders to partner with God in training the young.

Imagine a world where every child hears daily, “You are loved by God. You are chosen. You are capable. You are not alone.” Imagine classrooms where teachers pray quietly before lessons, workplaces where leaders model integrity, and homes where parents bless their children every morning. That is how nations change — one heart, one word, one seed at a time.

Old Testament Example:

When Joshua succeeded Moses, he carried not just authority but a spiritual inheritance. Moses had poured faith into him, mentoring him for years. So when the time came, Joshua could declare, *“As for me and my house, we will serve the Lord.”* (Joshua 24:15). That statement wasn’t born in a moment — it was built over years of being taught by a faithful leader.

New Testament Example:

The Apostle Paul poured into young Timothy, writing, *“And the things that you have heard from me among many witnesses, commit these to faithful men who will be able to teach others also.”* (2 Timothy 2:2). That is the divine relay — faith passed from one hand to the next, unbroken through generations.

Real-Life Example: The House of Daniels

In a quiet town, Mr. and Mrs. Daniels lived a simple life. They weren't rich or influential, but they understood the power of planting seeds. Every night, they gathered their three children — Nathan, Chloe, and Grace — for a brief time of prayer and Scripture. Even when work was hard and life demanding, they made this moment sacred.

When Nathan struggled with peer pressure in school, his father reminded him, *"Son, remember who you are. You're not called to fit in; you're called to stand out."*

When Chloe doubted her worth, her mother whispered over her, *"You are fearfully and wonderfully made."* (Psalm 139:14).

And when Grace once came home in tears after failing an exam, they prayed together, reminding her that failure was not final but formative.

Years passed. Nathan became a youth pastor, Chloe a school teacher, and Grace a nurse. None of them were perfect, but each carried the peace their parents had prayed for. Decades later, Mrs. Daniels was asked her secret. She smiled and said, *"We just kept planting. God did the growing."*

Faithfulness Is the True Measure of Success

In a world obsessed with outcomes, God looks for faithfulness. The faithful parent who prays when no one sees, the teacher who speaks life into weary students, the pastor who shepherds quietly, the grandparent who blesses their grandchildren — these are the heroes of heaven.

Jesus taught this principle clearly in the Parable of the Talents (Matthew 25:14–30). The reward was not given to the most talented but to the most faithful.

The Master said, *"Well done, good and faithful servant… you were faithful over a few things, I will make you ruler over many."* Faithfulness in small things brings divine increase.

In the Old Testament, Ruth's faithfulness to Naomi positioned her in the lineage of Christ (Ruth 1–4). She didn't chase greatness — she simply stayed true to love and loyalty. Faithfulness may seem unnoticed, but heaven records every act.

Real-Life Example:

Pastor James, a small-town minister, often wondered if his years of teaching children's Bible classes made any difference. One day, a young man named Aaron returned home and shared how those early lessons had shaped his faith and led him into ministry. With tears in his eyes, Pastor James realized that faithfulness never fails — it just takes time to bloom.

A Call to Action: Begin Today

The baton is in your hand now. Whether you are a parent, a teacher, a mentor, or a leader, God has entrusted you with lives to shape. Don't wait for the perfect time; begin today. Pray over your children. Teach them truth. Guide them in love. Bless them with your words.

Speak over them daily:

- ✓ *"You will fulfill your purpose."*
- ✓ *"You are chosen by God."*
- ✓ *"You will walk in wisdom and favor."*
- ✓ *"You will be a light in your generation."*

Every declaration you make becomes a prophetic brick in their foundation. The earlier you start, the stronger their spiritual structure will be.

Jesus began His ministry with a declaration from the Father:

"This is My beloved Son, in whom I am well pleased."
— Matthew 3:17
Before Jesus ever performed a miracle or preached a sermon, He was affirmed. That's the model for us — to bless and affirm before achievement. A child who knows they are loved will never need to search for validation elsewhere.

A Prophetic Vision Forward

Picture a generation that is fearless in faith, rooted in truth, and radiant with hope. A generation taught by the Lord, walking in peace, and led by His Spirit. That is not a dream — it is a promise.

Isaiah's prophecy is unfolding even now. God is raising children and youth who will be Daniels in a corrupt culture, Esthers in unjust systems, Josephs in economic spheres, and Timothys in spiritual leadership. But for that future to fully bloom, we must be faithful today.

Our greatest legacy will not be our achievements but our *investments in people*. The world may forget our names, but heaven will remember our seeds.

A Closing Prayer

Father, we thank You for entrusting us with the next generation. Teach us to be faithful sowers — patient, prayerful, and purposeful. Help us plant words of truth, nurture hearts with love, and water lives with Your Word. May our children be taught by You, walking in peace, power, and purpose. We declare that they will be builders in Your Kingdom, unshaken by the storms of life. And when You look upon our labor, may You find us faithful. In Jesus' name, Amen.

Appendices and Toolkits

1. Family Declarations & Blessing Prayers

Purpose:

To empower parents and guardians to speak daily life-giving words over their children, shaping identity, destiny, and confidence in God's Word.

How to Use:

- ✓ *Speak one declaration each morning or bedtime as a family.*
- ✓ *Parents can lay hands on their children while declaring.*
- ✓ *Encourage children to repeat them aloud in faith.*

Sample Daily Declarations (7-Day Cycle):

Day 1 – Identity

"I am fearfully and wonderfully made by God. I am His masterpiece."
(Psalm 139:14)

Prayer: *"Father, thank You that my child's identity is rooted in You. Let them grow in the confidence of who You created them to be."*

Day 2 – Purpose

"God has a special plan for my life, and I will walk in it boldly."
(Jeremiah 29:11)

Prayer: *"Lord, awaken the divine calling within my child. Order their steps toward Your purpose."*

Day 3 – Wisdom

"The Spirit of wisdom, understanding, and knowledge rests on me."
(Isaiah 11:2)

Prayer: *"Father, grant my child wisdom beyond their years to make godly decisions."*

Day 4 – Protection
"No weapon formed against me shall prosper."
(Isaiah 54:17)
Prayer: *"God, surround my child with Your angels and protect them from every snare of the enemy."*
Day 5 – Courage
"I am strong and courageous; I will not fear, for God is with me."
(Joshua 1:9)
Prayer: *"Lord, make my child bold in faith, standing strong in truth."*
Day 6 – Favor
"I have favor with God and with people."
(Luke 2:52)
Prayer: *"Father, open doors of divine favor and opportunity in my child's life."*
Day 7 – Faith
"I walk by faith, not by sight."
(2 Corinthians 5:7)
Prayer: *"Lord, let my child's faith grow daily, trusting You in every circumstance."*

Bonus Section:
"Our Family's Personalized Declarations" *for parents and children to write together.*
Day:
Bible Verse:
Prayer:

Day:
Bible Verse:
Prayer

Day:
Bible Verse:

Prayer

Day:
Bible Verse:
Prayer
...Continue doing so everyday!

---

2. 30-Day Family Devotional Plan

Purpose:
To help families cultivate a consistent devotional rhythm that deepens faith, love, and unity.
Format:
Each day includes a short *Bible verse*, *discussion prompt*, and *action step*.
Designed for 10–15 minutes daily.
Sample Structure (Week 1):
Day 1: *Genesis 1:27* – God Made Me Special
Talk About: What makes you unique?
Pray: Thank God for creating each person with purpose.
Do: Draw or write three special gifts God gave you.
Day 2: *Psalm 23:1* – God Takes Care of Me
Talk: How has God provided for us this week?
Do: Write one way to help someone else today.
Day 3: *Ephesians 4:32* – Be Kind
Talk: How can we show kindness in our home?
Do: Leave a thank-you note for a family member.
...and so on through 30 days, ending with:
Day 30: *Matthew 28:19–20* – Go and Share
Talk: How can our family show Jesus to others?
Do: Pray for one family we can bless this month.

---

3. Scripture Memory Cards for Kids

Purpose:

To help children hide God's Word in their hearts (Psalm 119:11).

Each card includes a verse, a declaration, and an action cue.

Design Concept:

Colorful, double-sided printable cards with illustrations or icons.

Example Cards:

Faith

"I can do all things through Christ who strengthens me." *(Philippians 4:13)*

Say: "I am strong because Jesus gives me strength."

Do: Try something new today and thank God for His help.

Love

"Love one another as I have loved you." *(John 15:12)*

Say: "I will love my friends and family like Jesus loves me."

Do: Share a kind word or gift today.

Courage

"When I am afraid, I put my trust in You." *(Psalm 56:3)*

Say: "I am brave because God is with me."

Do: Face something that scares you—pray first!

Obedience

"Children, obey your parents in the Lord." *(Ephesians 6:1)*

Say: "I will listen quickly and obey cheerfully."

Do: Help out before being asked.

---

4. “Faith at Home” Weekly Planner
Purpose:
To help parents structure weekly spiritual activities in a simple, family-friendly way.
Layout:
A one-page printable with sections for:
Memory Verse of the Week
Family Devotional Topic
Prayer Focus (e.g., “Our School,” “Grandparents,” “Nation”)
Faith in Action (service or kindness activity)
Worship Song of the Week
Family Night Idea
Sample Week Layout:
Week 3 Theme: *Walking in Love*
Memory Verse: Ephesians 5:2
Prayer Focus: Pray for classmates and teachers.
Faith in Action: Make handmade cards for someone who’s sick.
Worship Song: “Jesus Loves Me” (modern version)
Family Night: Movie + popcorn + talk about “How can we show love like Jesus?”
The planner can be reused weekly with different Scriptures and topics.

---

5. Church Children’s Ministry Strategy Template
Purpose:
To guide churches in developing a strong, Kingdom-driven ministry that equips and empowers children for lifelong faith.
Key Components:
a. Vision & Mission
Vision: *“To raise Spirit-filled children who know Jesus, walk in truth, and impact their world.”*

Mission Statement: *"Partnering with parents to disciple children through worship, Word, and works of service."*

b. Core Pillars

- ✓ **Discipleship over Entertainment** – *prioritize spiritual depth.*
- ✓ **Intergenerational Connection** – *involve parents, youth, and elders.*
- ✓ **Leadership Development** – *nurture young leaders early.*
- ✓ **Community Impact** – *encourage service and evangelism.*

c. Annual Planning Framework

Month	Focus Theme	Key Activity	Family Partnership
Jan	Identity in Christ	Vision Sunday for Kids	Parent prayer dedication
Apr	Resurrection Power	Easter Drama	Family outreach event
Jul	Missions & Service	Community Project	Family giving challenge
Oct	Word & Worship	Kids Bible Fair	Home devotion competition

d. Training for Teachers & Volunteers

- ✓ *Monthly spiritual formation sessions.*
- ✓ *Training on child psychology + biblical communication.*
- ✓ *Accountability groups for spiritual growth.*

e. Evaluation Tools

- ✓ *Quarterly feedback forms from parents.*
- ✓ *Spiritual milestone tracker (Salvation, Baptism, Service, Leadership).*

Final Encouragement

"You Are Building the Future Today"

"Every prayer whispered, every verse memorized, every seed sown into a child's heart carries eternal

weight. You are not merely raising a child — you are shaping a Kingdom warrior."

About the Author 'GERARD ASSEY'

Gerard Assey is a Graduate in Economics, a PGD in Management (HRD) and holds a Doctorate in Leadership. Gerard holds several International Qualifications in Sales, Debt Collection, Training & Teaching, and is a 'Fellow' of the prestigious 'Institute of Sales & Marketing Management'-UK, a Certified NLP Practitioner, a 'Certified Trainer', an 'Accredited Management Teacher-Behavioral Sciences', a 'Certified Competency Facilitator', a 'Certified Management Consultant'- (the International credentials of a professional management consultant, awarded in accordance with global standards of the ICMCI); and a Certification from the University of Michigan in 'Successful Negotiation: Essential Strategies and Skills'

He is also a Member of the 'National Association of Sales Professionals' backed with several years experience in varied industries, both in India and Overseas. He also holds an 'Etiquette Consultant' Certification from the USA (by Sue Fox, Author of Best Seller: 'Business Etiquette for Dummies'. She has trained some of the top celebrities' world over). He was also a recipient of a scholarship for extensive training in Japan on 'Corporate Management for India'.

Gerard Assey is 'Founder & Chief Corporate Trainer' of the Group: **'Citius, Altius, Fortius Unlimited'**- an organization that **celebrated 20 years of Glorious Service** in 2021, focusing on 3 Core Competencies:

People. Performance. Profit; in functional areas of Sales & Marketing, HR & Organizational Development, covering Recruitment, Training & Consultancy!

Having managed organizations with large Sales Forces in India & Overseas, his specialization cover extensive areas of Sales Training (All levels - Presentation, Negotiation, Key/ Strategic Accounts Management & Managerial Skills for all sectors), Bid Proposal/ Capture Planning/ Management Trainings, Retail Sales, Customer Service & Customer Retention Programs, Training for Prevention & Collection of Debt, Self & Personal Development Programs (Time Management, Teamwork & Team Building, Business Etiquette & Personal Grooming, Leadership & Managerial Skills, People Management Skills, Train-the-Trainer etc), including preparation of Custom-designed Business Manuals for Internal (HR, Induction, and Sales etc) & External use (Instruction, User Manuals).

Gerard has successfully conducted over 6480 Trainings & Workshops (as of Sept '25) all across India, Middle East, Africa, Europe & S.E. Asia. Besides public programs conducted regularly, both in India & Overseas, he has some of the top names as clients whom he services from Single Owners to large Public & Government undertakings, covering all sectors, for their in-house needs.

His website: www.CollectionSkills.com is the only one in this part of the world to be featured in the 'Collections & Credit Risk Magazine-USA' under 'Who's Who in Training' and ranks TOP, along with other websites listed below on most search engines.

Gerard is author of 207 Books already (Oct 2025), all the books being available on all online platforms and outlets as E-books and Paperbacks

A few of our business related books:

1. Bite-sized Bits on Commonsense Management
2. Heart to Heart on Life's Principles'
3. How to become a Successful Manager
4. The Sales Professionals' Master Workbook of S.Y.S.T.E.M.S
5. The Professional Business Email Etiquette Handbook & Guide
6. The Professional Business Video-Conferencing Etiquette Handbook & Guide
7. Professional Presentation Skills
8. Exceptional Customer Service
9. Professional Tele-Marketing Skills
10. Professional Debt Collection Skills
11. The G.R.E.A.T. Sales & Service Workbook
12. Sales Training Advantage for Results (*The Ultimate Sales Training Manual to enable you stand out as a S.T.A.R.*)
13. CEO Daily Planner & Organizer
14. The Sales Professionals' Master Daily Planner
15. The Professional Debt Collector's Master Daily Planner
16. My Daily Planner & Organizer
17. MY EMERGENCY INFORMATION RECORD (Family Emergency & Peace of Mind Planner)
18. The Ultimate Therapist & Counselors Planner and Organizer
19. Building an Ethical Workplace
20. Managing Relationships at Work
21. Managing Business Meetings Effectively
22. Effective Delegation Skills
23. Goal Setting for Success
24. B2B Selling by Email
25. Professional Business Etiquette & Grooming
26. Dining Etiquette & Table Manners
27. Effective Networking Skills
28. Grooming, Etiquette & Manners for Teens, Young Adults & Future Leaders
29. Inter-Personal Skills
30. Get Ready, Get Hired!
31. Selling in a Recession
32. Effective Receivables Management in an Economic Downturn!
33. Real Estate & Property Sales Training
34. Credit Sales & Accounts Receivable Management

35. Selling Skills for Real Estate & Property Advisors
36. Take G.R.E.A.T. C.A.R.E!
37. Spa, Salon & Health Club Selling Skills
38. Selling Travel, Holiday & MICE Services
39. Selling Skills for Spa's, Salons & Health Clubs
40. Retailing in Salons & Spas
41. Selling Holiday, Vacation, Tours & Packages
42. The Power of Sales Referrals
43. Selling Luxury
44. Technical Selling Skills
45. Financial Advisors Sales Training
46. Dealing with Burnout at Work Monopolize Your Markets
47. Selling to Affluent Customers
48. Growing up with Grace
49. Financial Selling Skills
50. *The Effective Manager's Guide: Key Skills to Thrive*
51. From Aspiring to Inspiring: A Guide for New Managers on the Rise
52. The Power of Focus
53. Selling with Integrity: Sell Like Jesus The Perfect Role Model!
54. 31 Habits of Champions: Your 31-Day Journey to Greatness
55. Rejecting Grasshopper Talk: From Grasshopper to Giant-Killer-*Defeating Giants Daily!*
56. Navigate the AI-Powered Future of Bid & Proposals: Up-Skill to Stay Relevant with Alternative Career Paths & Opportunities
57. Hiring Sales Winners
58. Present with Impact
59. Success Unlocked: *Breaking Free from Habits that Hold You Back*
60. Complaints to Cheers, Feedback to Gold: Mastering Complaints Management
61. Thriving Together: *Cultivating Diversity, Equity, and Inclusion*
62. Coaching Skills for Sales Managers
63. Soaring to Success in Business & Leadership: Swifter, Higher, Stronger!
64. From Classroom to Podium: A Student's Guide to Powerful Public Speaking & Presentation Skills
65. Developing Self-Discipline
66. The CEO's 31-Day Power Plan: Unlocking Success through Essential Traits

67. Credibility Matters
68. A Winning Attitude
69. Bid & Proposal Management Using AI
70. Sales Forecasting: A Practical & Proven Guide to Strategic Sales Forecasting
71. Elevate & Energize: *50 Dynamic & Fun Activities for Peak Workplace Morale*
72. 'Sales SOS! Sales on Fire! *30 Days to Conquer Chaos & the Nightmares of Success!'*
73. Mastering Sales Managerial Skills: *Building High-Performing Teams & Driving Exceptional Results*
74. Eagle-Eyed Leadership: Unleashing the Power of 31 Lessons from Eagles
75. The Ultimate Employee Training Guide: *Training Today, Leading Tomorrow*
76. Being More Accountable at Work
77. Creating a Culture of Continuous Improvement
78. Effective Questioning & Listening Skills
79. The Power of Value Selling
80. The Growth Mindset
81. Mastering Professional Help Desk Skills
82. The Power to Lead with Empathy
83. Being Prepared: The Key to Unlocking Success
84. Youthful Spark-Youth Energizers, Activities and Games-Igniting the Fun in Youth
85. Ignite your Motivation for Success
86. Elevate Your Executive Presence: *Your Roadmap to Executive Excellence*
87. Smart Decisions: *Mastering Problem Solving with Strategic Solutions for Business Success*
88. Strategic Planning: *Developing and Implementing Strategic Plans to Achieve Long-Term Business Goals*
89. The Power of Stay Interviews
90. Developing G.R.I.T.
91. Adaptability
92. Diagnosis- *A Key Skill for Leadership*
93. The Burnout-Proof Salesperson: *The Master Guide to Preventing Stress & Burnout*- Strategies for Thriving in Sales
94. Learning from Failure: *Keys to Success*
95. Customer Success Management
96. Overcoming the Killers of Motivation
97. The C-Suite Code: *Mastering Skills for Executive Excellence'*

98. Dealing with Difficult Customers
99. Unlocking Your Potential: Mastering the Top 20 Life Skills for a Brighter Future
100. Nurturing Tomorrow's Leaders: *Essential Soft Skills Every Child Must Learn*
101. Lively & Fun Party Games for Seniors & Elders
102. Role Playing for Sales Champions: From Practice to Performance
103. Fun and Exciting Party Games for Kids
104. Case Studies for Sales
105. Role-Playing for Unbeatable Customer Service
106. Case Studies in Customer Service
107. Case Studies in Winning Negotiations
108. Case Studies in Management & Leadership
109. Case Studies in Human Resources & Talent Management
110. CEO Success Blueprint: The Essential Toolkit for CEOs and C-Level Executives
111. The Salesperson's Self-Coaching Guide: *Master Your Own Self-Coaching Plan for Success*
112. Overcoming Procrastination: *Your Ultimate Guide to Stop Delaying and Start Living Your Best Life*
113. When True Colors Are Exposed: *The Journey to Unmasking Humanity*
114. Life-Changing Habits for Teens: Teen Success Blueprint for a Bright Future
115. Workplace Stress-Free: *Proven Strategies to Thrive at Work and Beyond*
116. Objection Overruled: *The Ultimate Guide to Turning 'No' into 'Yes'*
117. Building Strong Teams: *A Comprehensive Guide to Team Building*
118. Ethical & Moral Leadership in Business: *Eliminating Unethical Practices & Building a Culture of Trust & Integrity*
119. Rising Strong: Building Positive: High Self-Esteem for a Fulfilling Life-*A Practical Guide for Students, Employees, Leaders & Entrepreneurs*
120 The Cheerful Mindset: Cultivating a Joyful Outlook Everyday
121. Leading Through Crisis: Case Studies on Crisis Management

From the Ministry side, Gerard graduated in the very first batch of Charis Bible College-India & had for over 9 years served as a Part-time Faculty at Charis Bible College-Chennai (Andrew Wommack Ministries-Colorado, USA).
He also holds a Diploma in Worship (a subject closest to his heart) from the JSOW and is also a graduate of the Advanced Mentorship Program (AMP) and the Circle Of Ministerial Engagement (C.O.M.E.) of Prophet Jerome Fernando and a Spiritual Son of the Esteemed Prophet.
An accomplished author of several Secular & Christian Books, Gerard has been on the board of a few international organizations and boasts of being the SON of the MOST HIGH GOD: An ordinary guy following an extraordinary GOD!

...And some of his most recent Christian Books being:

1. A Bouquet of Praises for My KING
2. Christian Jokes for the Serious Religious' Folks!
3. Jesus Healed You!
4. Praise24Ever! (also in Tamil version)
5. The 5G Network of GOD
6. Building Faith over F.E.A.R- FACE EVERYTHING AND RISE with JESUS
7. Hebrew and Greek Praise and Worship Words
8. Godly Mothers' and Grandmothers' Bible Story time for Kids!
9. Miracles of Jesus in Pictures
10. Raise your Praise all 365 Days
11. Thanking GOD with an Attitude of Gratitude
12. Meditating on the Attributes of GOD
13. Puppet Scripts
14. Alcohol Ruins, JESUS Reforms, Renews & Restores!
15. Habakkuk 2:2 Christian Daily Journal, Planner & Organizer
16. ABC of GOD's Word for Handwriting Practice
17. Daily Bible Verse Handwriting Practice (Building Godly Character & Faith through Cursive Handwriting Practice!)
18. Guiding Light: Fun & Faith-Building Bible Activities for Children
19. Rejecting Grasshopper Talk: From Grasshopper to Giant-Killer-*Defeating Giants Daily!*
20. Teen Titans of Faith: *Building Courage, Determination & Christ-like-Esteem*
21. I AM Empowered: *Unleashing Divine Power with Positive*

Declarations

22. Be A Solution Provider-*From Passion to Purpose*: *A Biblical Guide to Being the Answer to the World!*
23. Miracles of JESUS
24. Parables of Jesus for a Meaningful Life!
25. A Grateful Heart: Importance of Sharing Testimonies of GOD's Grace
26. Melodies of Worship to JESUS: 31 Songs of Praise & Worship From My Heart to HIS!
27. I AM SO BLESSED!
28. My Daily Cup of Energizer
29. 31 Leadership Lessons *from* Jesus- *The Supreme Leader*
30. Peace Amidst Storms: A Biblical Guide to Conquering S.T.R.E.S.S.
31. Rise Above: 20 Biblical Eagle Lessons for Life's Triumphs
32. Godly Goal Setting: *The FAITHFUL Blueprint for a Purpose-Driven Life*
33. The Profound Attributes of our Mighty GOD: Understanding the 10S's of the Almighty
34. Worship Now, Worship Forever: *A Journey from Earthly Praise to Eternal Glory*
35. Unceasing Praise & Worship: *365 Days to Worship the King*
36. The ROAR Within: *Living with Purpose and Authority through the Power of the Holy Spirit*
37. From Potential to Purpose: Unlocking and Multiplying Your Talents & Gifts for Kingdom Impact
38. Songs from the Heart: *Worshipping GOD in Your Own Tune & Melody*
39. Awakening Praise & Worship: Hebrew & Greek Words to Raise Your Praise
40. Sing a NEW Song to the LORD Everyday: *Daily Devotions of Praise & Worship to Lift Your Heart & Glorify HIS Name*
41. *The* A.R.O.M.A. of True Worship: *Creating Worship That Delights God*
42. Becoming A Kingdom Champion: *Embracing God's Call for a Life of Purpose & Victory*
43. The Busy Businessman's Daily Devotional: 366 Crisp Truths to Start Your Day Strong
44. The Teacher's Heart: *Daily Devotions for Educators*
45. Anchored! *A 31-Day Devotional for Students Facing Life's Challenges*
46. Suddenly! Unlocking Unorthodox Breakthroughs through Unusual Worship

47. Overcoming Adversity: *Lessons from the Bible for Modern Challenges*
48. LORD, Don't do it without me
49. Kingdom Leadership: *Biblical Principles for Modern Leaders*
50. Heartprints of God- *Growing God's Way:* Daily Devotions for Kids to Shine Bright
51. Send Judah First: Let your Praises Go up First to See the Mighty Move of GOD
52. DIVINE MOMENTS: *Recognizing, Embracing, Preparing, and Walking into Life-Changing Encounters with God*
53. Be a Builder in the Kingdom: *The C.E.M.E.N.T. Guide to Creating a Lasting Legacy*
54. Unshakable: *Pillars of Godly Womanhood* (Pillars of Faith That Changed History)
55. Lead Like a Shepherd: *14 Essential Traits for Pastoral Excellence*
56. The Worship Leader's Arsenal: *Powerful Exhortations to Ignite Thanksgiving, Praise & Worship*
57. Women of UnShakable Faith: *31-Day Devotional for Strength, Purpose & Influence*
58. Called to Teach: *A Complete 10-Week Training Guide for Impactful VBS Teachers*
59. Strumming for the KING: Cowboy Songs of Faith & Fire
60. The Ultimate Youth Camp Playbook: *50 Bible-Centered Indoor Games to Engage, Equip, and Empower Teens*
61. Glad in HIS Presence: *David's Revelation of GOD's Love & Mercy*
62. The Spirit Behind the Sound: *52 Devotionals for Worship Teams*
63. THE COWBOY'S COMPASS: *Riding the Trail of Faith with Grit & Grace*
64. Worship as My Weapon: *Living Victoriously through the Power of Praise*
65. A Worshipper Always Wins*: Living a Life of Victorious Worship*
66. Worship That Leads to the Throne: *Practical Strategies for Worship Leaders to Inspire Their Team & Usher People into God's Presence*
67. Worship as Warfare: *Conquering through the Sound of Surrender*
68. Watchmen on the Walls: *A 31-Day Devotional for Worship Teams*

69. KINGDOM BUSINESS: *52 Biblical Principles for GODLY Leadership & Wise Decisions*
70. From Evening to Morning: *Rediscovering GOD's Sacred Hours*
71. Waves of Glory: *Worship through Dance, Flags, Staff & Sound*
72. WORSHIP TEAM BUILDER: *Guiding Your Team from Formation to Fruitfulness*
73. The Worship Leader's Master Training Manual
74. Skits for the King: Children's Plays for Every Church Occasion
75. Unbreakable: Building Strong Marriages and Families God's Way *(From Vows to Victory)*
76. Songs for my King: *A 31-Day Journey of Praise*
77. Building Powerful Children: *Raising a Generation That Will Shape the Future for God*

Besides regularly contributing to business & trade journals, including international ones such as the 'Creative Training Techniques' and the 'Sales News' of the U.S.A, He is also a member of several prestigious bodies & trade associations, having participated in many Conferences & Workshops in India & Overseas.

Prior to his last assignment of leading & managing a large MNC as head, Gerard had a 3-year stint in the Middle East as a Consultant with a leading British Consultancy Firm.

As the past 'Official Country Representative' for the International Business Award- 'THE STEVIES'-(the business world's own Oscar) for about 4 years- he ensured a few Indian companies that qualify for the same every year!

Gerard can be contacted at:
Email: training@Sales-Training.in,training@CollectionSkills.com
Websites:

www.Sales-Training.in
www.EtiquetteWorks.in
www.CollectionSkills.com
www.RetailSalesTraining.in
www.SalesTrainingIndia.com
www.ManualPreparation.com
www.TrainingWithPuppets.com
www.FirstContactAcademy.com
www.SalesAndMarketingRecruiter.com

www.ingramcontent.com/pod-product-compliance
Ingram Content Group UK Ltd.
Pitfield, Milton Keynes, MK11 3LW, UK
UKHW021340190726
13845UKWH00027B/646

9 788199 301757